BUILDING A MORE RESILIENT HAITIAN STATE

Keith Crane, James Dobbins, Laurel E. Miller,
Charles P. Ries, Christopher S. Chivvis,
Marla C. Haims, Marco Overhaus,
Heather Lee Schwartz, Elizabeth Wilke

Sponsored by the Carnegie Corporation of New York
and the Smith Richardson Foundation

RAND NATIONAL SECURITY
RESEARCH DIVISION

The research described in this report was sponsored by the Carnegie Corporation of New York and the Smith Richardson Foundation and was conducted within the International Security and Defense Policy Center of the RAND National Security Research Division.

Library of Congress Cataloging-in-Publication Data

Building a more resilient Haitian state / Keith Crane ... [et al.].
p. cm.
Includes bibliographical references.
ISBN 978-0-8330-5043-4 (pbk. : alk. paper)
1. Political planning—Haiti. 2. Nation-building—Haiti. 3. Haiti—Politics and government—1986- I. Crane, Keith, 1953- II. Rand Corporation.

JL1089.5.P64B85 2010
320.6097294--dc22

2010031440

Cover photos by The Miami Herald, *used with permission*

Published 2010 by the RAND Corporation
1776 Main Street, P.O. Box 2138, Santa Monica, CA 90407-2138
1200 South Hayes Street, Arlington, VA 22202-5050
4570 Fifth Avenue, Suite 600, Pittsburgh, PA 15213-2665
RAND URL: http://www.rand.org/
To order RAND documents or to obtain additional information, contact
Distribution Services: Telephone: (310) 451-7002;
Fax: (310) 451-6915; Email: order@rand.org

Preface

This report appraises past and current plans and policies to improve the provision of public services in Haiti and, drawing on this appraisal, provides recommendations on how those plans and policies might be improved. The report focuses on setting priorities and suggesting how programs and initiatives might be refocused so as to provide palpable improvements in the provision of public services in Haiti over the course of the next few years. It is designed to be useful to the government of Haiti as it develops detailed plans for policy and institutional reforms and to the international donor community as it determines how to support the government's efforts.

The research described in this report was sponsored by the Carnegie Corporation of New York and the Smith Richardson Foundation and was conducted within the International Security and Defense Policy Center of the RAND National Security Research Division (NSRD). NSRD conducts research and analysis for the Office of the Secretary of Defense, the Joint Staff, the Unified Combatant Commands, the defense agencies, the Navy, the Marine Corps, the U.S. Coast Guard, the U.S. Intelligence Community, allied foreign governments, and foundations.

For more information on RAND's International Security and Defense Policy Center, contact the Director, James Dobbins. He can be reached by email at James_Dobbins@rand.org; by phone at 703-413-1100, extension 5134; or by mail at the RAND Corporation, 1200 S. Hayes Street, Arlington, VA 22202. More information about RAND is available at www.rand.org.

Contents

Figures

Summary

In addition to demonstrating the weaknesses of Haiti's infrastructure, the earthquake that struck Haiti on January 12, 2010, exposed the weaknesses of Haiti's state institutions. To avoid a repetition of the disaster, the government of Haiti and the international donor community now need to turn to building the foundations for a more effective state.

Daunting as the current challenges are—acute problems layered on chronic ones—the need for reconstruction and the likely infusion of funding from external sources open up the possibility of creating a new basis for stability and economic growth. Following the change of government in 2004 came five consecutive years of economic growth and tentative progress toward better governance. This progress indicates that, with better policies, Haiti can recover from the effects of the earthquake and embark on a period of improved public security, social well-being, and sustained economic growth.

Prior to the earthquake, the government of Haiti broadly articulated its strategy for pursuing development and improving governance in its *Growth and Poverty Reduction Strategy Paper* (GPRSP) of 2007.[1] Building on that paper, a general strategy for reforming Haiti's economy was approved at an April 2009 donors' conference in Washington, D.C.[2] After the 2010 earthquake, the government prepared its *Action*

[1] Republic of Haiti (2008).

[2] This donors' conference followed a series of damaging hurricanes and tropical storms that struck Haiti in 2008.

Plan for National Recovery and Development of Haiti,[3] which it presented at a donors' conference held in New York in March 2010.

These documents provide a vision for Haiti's reconstruction and development and identify funding needs. However, they do not provide a comprehensive, critical examination of preexisting plans in all sectors that takes into account the need to put state-building at the forefront of efforts to ignite progress. They often fail to set realistic goals and priorities; these failures risk squandering resources and, more importantly, the opportunity to set right deeply embedded problems.

The purpose of this report is to fill this gap by appraising past and current plans to improve public-service provision in Haiti and, drawing on these appraisals, providing recommendations to improve those plans. The report focuses on setting priorities for the next few years and suggesting measures that might produce palpable improvements in the provision of public services during this time frame. The report is designed to be useful to the government of Haiti as it develops detailed plans for policy and institutional reforms and to the international donor community as it determines how to support the government's efforts.

For each of the core state functions addressed in this report, we describe the principal challenges; appraise the relevant plans, policies, and initiatives; and offer recommendations, focusing on the highest priorities. We have set common criteria for the recommendations: that they be fiscally sustainable, commensurate with the administrative capacity of Haiti's government; realistic in their prospects for implementation; geared toward enhancing the effectiveness of the Haitian state; and mutually coherent. We have focused on recommending actions that could commence quickly and yield positive outcomes within the next three to five years. This summary highlights our most important recommendations.

---

[3] Republic of Haiti (2010a).

Governance and Public Administration

Together with limited financial resources, the lack of skilled, trained, and properly organized government personnel and the lack of management systems within ministries and other government bodies are the principal constraints on the state's effectiveness. The implications of the institutional deficiencies in planning, budgeting, executing policy decisions, and managing people and resources cut across all the government activities covered in this report, including the government's ability to interact with donors. Some of the most essential changes needed to strengthen the Haitian state will require legislation, or even constitutional change.

Key Recommendations

- Provide sufficient donor funding to implement a reformulated strategy for administrative reform based on *Programme-Cadre de Réforme de l'Etat: Modernisation Administrative et Décentralisation, 2007–2012*, to which we refer in this report as the *framework program*.[4]
- Within this strategy, civil service reform deserves the highest priority. Key steps include creating job descriptions; establishing standards and procedures for hiring and firing; creating a system for merit-based promotions; setting competitive, fiscally responsible salary grades; and providing incentives tied to achieving concrete, independently monitored performance targets.
- Major donors need to employ their considerable influence in concerted, carefully focused, discreet, and subtle ways to promote the political reforms essential to any broader program of state-building.

---

4 Republic of Haiti (2007).

Justice

Haiti's justice system is deeply flawed: The courts do not carry out their constitutional responsibilities; laws are not applied and procedures are not followed; the criminal code dates from the early 19th century; prison conditions are horrific; an accused has almost no access to legal advice if he or she cannot afford to pay for a lawyer; legal professionals are often poorly educated; corruption is widespread; and relations are poor between the Haitian National Police (HNP) on the one hand and prosecutors and judges on the other. The various plans and initiatives to address these problems that have been developed since the mid-1990s have borne very little fruit.

Key Recommendations

- With assistance from donors, the Haitian government needs to create and implement a comprehensive system for managing cases that links the police, prosecutors, judges, and prisons.
- The Haitian government should create a special pretrial detainee review mechanism to resolve the large number of cases of illegally prolonged detention.
- The Haitian government, with donor support, should establish a property-dispute resolution mechanism. Putting in place an accelerated procedure for determining asset ownership is essential to reducing obstacles to reconstruction and economic activity. In conjunction with this, work that is under way to address serious gaps in birth, death, and identity registration should be completed expeditiously.

Security

Efforts to reform the security sector in Haiti have faced three main, related challenges: the volatile security situation and the limited ability of the state to assert its authority, the lack of consistent government commitment to police reform, and the low level of institutional development within the HNP.

In mid-2006, when police reform began in earnest, the HNP consisted of just 7,000 badly equipped, poorly trained officers. The HNP lacked the abilities to keep records on current and former police officers, manage its finances, and set and enforce internal controls. Low salaries and poor working conditions for the majority of police officers contributed to corruption and criminal activity within the force. Though progress, especially in recruitment, training, and vetting, has been made, the HNP still lacks the capacity to respond effectively to Haiti's internal security threats without external assistance.

Key Recommendations

- Providing public security must remain at the forefront of the Haitian government's priorities. The Haitian government and the international community should agree to keep United Nations (UN) peacekeepers for at least the next five years and to then reduce the international military and police presence only gradually.
- The government of Haiti and donors should focus on building the HNP's administrative capacity.

Economic Policy

Haiti's primary economic challenge is generating economic growth. It is the poorest country in the Western Hemisphere, with a per capita income of less than one-quarter of the average for Latin America and the Caribbean. Haiti is poor in great part because of its difficult environment for business. The process of registering a business is one of the most complex and lengthy in the world and is relatively costly. Registering changes in title for property is even more onerous. The difficulties Haitians face in engaging in economic activity have stifled economic development.

Key Recommendations

- To accelerate economic growth, the Haitian government should quickly eliminate unnecessary procedures involved in registering businesses and property and reduce the cost and length of time needed to complete the remaining steps.

Housing and Infrastructure

The earthquake had a devastating effect on housing in Haiti. Although the tent cities have been an effective stopgap measure, providing permanent housing for the displaced is urgent because the hurricane season has begun. In addition, infrastructure (roads, ports, airports, electric-power system, water, and sewage) will need to be improved and maintained if Haiti is to enjoy sustained economic growth and the health and well-being of its citizens are to improve. Expanding infrastructure is not just a question of building new highways and power plants. Systems are required for maintaining infrastructure once built and, as importantly, for ensuring that utilities charge and collect enough revenues to cover the costs of services they provide. In many respects, the current parlous state of Haiti's infrastructure is due more to the failure to ensure that infrastructure is well maintained and operated than to lack of money for the construction of new projects.

Key Recommendations

- The Haitian government, together with the donor community, should accelerate removal of rubble. This is the single most important step toward reconstruction of housing and infrastructure that the Haitian government and donors can take.
- The Haitian government should eliminate restrictions on the operations of private container ports.
- To ensure that electric power is available for businesses and households, the Haitian government should move to full cost-recovery pricing and decentralize and enforce collection of bills owed.

Education

Overall low quality, lack of access, and little oversight characterize the country's education sector. As a result, Haiti has no coherent system of education. Enrollment rates and levels of educational attainment are low; although many children experience *some* schooling in episodic spells, an alarming number do not obtain a complete basic education. The 2008 hurricanes and the 2010 earthquake greatly exacerbated the weaknesses in education. In addition to the effects on students and teachers, more than 80 percent of school buildings in Port-au-Prince were destroyed.

Key Recommendations

- To help close the gap in quality between private and public schools and to increase access to schools, the Ministry of Education and Training (Ministère de l'Education Nationale et de la Formation Professionnelle, or MENFP) should subsidize private-school teacher wages to be on par with those of public-school teachers. These subsidies should be conditioned on teaching in an accredited school that charges capped (minimal) fees to families.

Health

Approximately 40 percent of Haitians lack access (both physical and financial) to health care, particularly in rural areas of the country. Many health-care facilities are outdated, and much of the medical equipment is old or broken. The Ministry of Public Health and Population (Ministère de la Santé Publique et de la Population, or MSPP) does not have systems in place to track health status and monitor quality of care and has little human capital or administrative capacity to carry out its functions. A lack of not only doctors and nurses but also administrative professionals has been a major challenge. Prior to the earthquake, the health sector was receiving the largest amount of foreign aid of all service sectors in Haiti. Such extensive donor involvement has created a management challenge for the government that it has been unable to overcome: the need to coordinate, regulate, and oversee the plans and activities of donors and local nongovernmental organizations (NGOs) engaged in health-care delivery in Haiti.

Key Recommendations

- In light of the MSPP's lack of capacity and funding, it should shift the operation of all health centers and hospitals to NGOs and other private institutions. The MSPP should establish a performance-based contracting mechanism for these operations and the provision of health services throughout the country.

Donor Cooperation

As the poorest country in the hemisphere and the only one that has experienced a decline in per capita gross domestic product (GDP) over the past three decades, Haiti has been a focus of concern for donors of humanitarian and development assistance for two generations. Despite a major commitment of donor resources, Haiti's economic, social, and political situation has worsened. The January 2010 earthquake has been followed by an extraordinary increase in promised resources for and attention to the international effort to assist Haiti's recovery and long-term development. As the response to the disaster took shape, donors and the Haitian government adopted the slogan "building back better." The government's postearthquake action plan[5] presents a new-to-Haiti architecture for managing the large flows of assistance pledged at the March 2010 donors' conference. A key element is the creation of a short-term joint Haitian government/donor commission, the Interim Haiti Recovery Commission (IHRC).[6]

---

5 Republic of Haiti (2010a).

6 Earlier, the IHRC was referred to as the Interim Haiti Reconstruction Commission. For current information regarding the IHRC, see IHRC (undated).

Key Recommendations

- Donors should focus on making the IHRC an effective body by agreeing that all major donors, including the United States, will submit all project and program concepts to the IHRC for coordination and will adapt them in accordance with Haiti's and other donors' plans and preferences. If donors and the government do not use the IHRC to make decisions, the commission may become no more than an information exchange.
- The United States, as the largest bilateral contributor, should better organize itself to engage politically with the Haitian government through appointment of a full-time, high-ranking special coordinator or envoy. Similarly, a handful of major bilateral and multilateral donors should organize themselves for more-coordinated political engagement with Haiti's leaders through the creation of a "friends" or "contact" group for Haiti.

Conclusion

Hope for a more prosperous and peaceful future for the Haitian people lies in building a more effective, resilient state. The discussions of challenges throughout this report show that Haiti's state institutions are riddled with weaknesses in the areas of human resources, organization, procedures, and policies. The appraisals of reform plans and initiatives in this report acknowledge that devising lists of measures needed to repair the state's weaknesses is relatively easy but that formulating strategies to address those weaknesses is hard—and implementation is even harder.

This report supports the development of a Haitian state-building strategy by recommending how to build on existing plans for improving institutions and the delivery of public services and by proposing state-building priorities. Plans that do not set priorities and detail sequencing and responsibilities are unlikely to have much impact on government policymaking and donor funding decisions. If priorities are not set, the government's ability to carry out any plans is compromised. And broad plans with an abundance of objectives enable donors to justify whatever projects they wish to fund, leading to incoherent donor interventions.

The priorities proposed in this report are based on what is necessary, feasible, and sustainable by the Haitian government over the long term. Among the many desirable reforms and initiatives, these changes stand out as meriting the greatest degree of political and policy attention by the government of Haiti and donors, as well as full funding.

While this report focuses on practical steps that can be taken to strengthen Haiti's state institutions, it should not be read as implying that state-building is a purely technical process. State-building is intimately connected with politics. Without executive decisiveness and legislative action, state-building cannot proceed. Thus, a considerable burden rests on the shoulders of Haiti's political leaders, who will need to rise to the challenge of overcoming a history of fractiousness, patronage, and indecision. Donors and international organizations can help ease that burden—not only by providing financial resources but also by promoting political consensus and encouraging adherence to strategic plans.

Acknowledgments

We are grateful to Stephen Del Rosso of the Carnegie Corporation of New York and Marin Strmecki of the Smith Richardson Foundation for supporting this work. We benefited greatly from the insights and observations of numerous Haitian government officials, representatives of multilateral and bilateral donors, and nongovernmental experts on Haiti, including participants in workshops we conducted in Haiti and at RAND. We thank U.S. Ambassador to Haiti Kenneth Merten and his staff at the U.S. Embassy in Port-au-Prince for their help, especially in regard to our research visits to Haiti, and Alice Nkunzimana for her excellent interpretation and other on-the-ground support. Our RAND colleague Howard Shatz and Charles Call of American University provided valuable comments in their reviews of our draft report. Finally, we thank Sean Halpin, Jennifer Miller, and Joy Merck for providing important administrative support.

Abbreviations

AECID	Agencia Española de Cooperación Internacional para el Desarrollo
AFD	Agence Française de Développement
AIDS	acquired immunodeficiency syndrome
BHSP	Basic Health Services Package
BOT	build-operate-transfer
BRH	Bank of the Republic of Haiti
CAMEP	Centrale Autonome Métropolitaine d'Eau Potable
CARICOM	Caribbean Community
CIDA	Canadian International Development Agency
DAC	Development Assistance Committee (of the Organisation for Economic Co-Operation and Development)
DAP	Direction Administrative Pénitentiaire, or Directorate of Penitentiary Administration
DEC	Disasters Emergency Committee
DPT	diphtheria-pertussis-tetanus
EdH	Électricité d'Haïti

EFA	Education for All
EU	European Union
FER	Fonds d'Entretien Routier, or Road Maintenance Fund
FMIS	financial management information system
FTI	Fast Track Initiative
GDP	gross domestic product
GPRSP	Growth and Poverty Reduction Strategy Paper
HDA	Haitian Development Authority
HIV	human immunodeficiency virus
HNP	Haitian National Police
HOPE Act II	Haitian Hemispheric Opportunity Through Partnership Encouragement Act II
ICF	Interim Cooperation Framework
ICRC	International Committee of the Red Cross
IDA	International Development Agency
IDB	Inter-American Development Bank
IHRC	Interim Haiti Recovery Commission
IMF	International Monetary Fund
ISDR	United Nations International Strategy for Disaster Reduction
M&E	monitoring and evaluation
MDG	Millennium Development Goal
MDTF	multidonor trust fund

MENFP	Ministère de l'Education Nationale et de la Formation Professionnelle, or Ministry of Education and Training
MINUSTAH	Mission des Nations Unies pour la Stabilisation en Haïti, or United Nations Stabilization Mission in Haiti
MJSP	Ministère de la Justice et de la Sécurité Publique, or Ministry of Justice and Public Security
MSPP	Ministère de la Santé Publique et de la Population, or Ministry of Public Health and Population
NGO	nongovernmental organization
OAS	Organization of American States
OCHA	Office for the Coordination of Humanitarian Affairs (of the United Nations)
OECD	Organisation for Economic Co-Operation and Development
OMRH	Office de Management et des Ressources Humaines, or Office of Human Resources Management
PAHO	Pan American Health Organization
PDNA	postdisaster needs assessment
POCHEP	Poste Communautaire d'Hygiène et d'Eau Potable
PRGF	Poverty Reduction and Growth Facility
SNEP	Service National d'Eau Potable
START	Stabilization and Reconstruction Task Force
TB	tuberculosis

UCS	unité communale de santé, or community health unit
UN	United Nations
UNCTAD	United Nations Conference on Trade and Development
UNDP	United Nations Development Programme
UNESCO	United Nations Educational, Scientific and Cultural Organization
UNICEF	United Nations Children's Fund
USAID	U.S. Agency for International Development
VAT	value-added tax
WHO	World Health Organization

CHAPTER ONE

Introduction

On January 12, 2010, an earthquake devastated Port-au-Prince, Léogâne, and other cities and settlements in the south of Haiti, leaving 300,000 people dead, another 300,000 injured, and 1.3 million homeless. The Haitian government and the international community moved rapidly to address the immediate humanitarian crisis. The homeless are now sheltered in tents and provided with food and water. The airport was quickly reopened, and the port of Port-au-Prince has been returned to service. Much has stabilized in Haiti, although the threat looms of a severe hurricane season that may devastate the tent cities in which so many Haitians now live.

Although the earthquake was the cause of the disaster, Haiti's long history of poor government was largely responsible for the extent of the devastation and the society's almost complete dependence on help from abroad to deal with the consequences. The earthquake thus demonstrated not only the weaknesses of Haiti's physical infrastructure but also the more fundamental weaknesses of its institutions. The massive loss of life and infrastructure was, in great part, due to poor-quality construction materials and methods, enabled by lack of oversight and accountability. The difficulties relief agencies faced in getting to damaged sites and rescuing victims was compounded by Haiti's poor roads, ports, and airports. Given its location, Haiti cannot avoid frequent hurricanes and occasional earthquakes, but the scale of the resultant devastation can be reduced and the robustness of the response improved. To do so, the government of Haiti and the international donor community now need to turn to laying the foundations of an effective state—one that can build and maintain infrastructure and deliver public services better than before January 12, as well as more generally improve the lives of the Haitian people.

Daunting as the current challenges are—acute problems layered on chronic ones—the need for reconstruction and the likelihood of an infusion of international resources to fund it open up the possibility of laying a new foundation for stability and economic growth. Though the earthquake has once again laid bare the fragility of the Haitian state, Haiti has many advantages compared to other fragile states:

- It is not part of a troubled region with unhelpful neighbors.
- It has no intractable ethnic or other structural divides.
- Many of its government officials have the will, if not the resources, to improve their country's circumstances.
- The Haitian diaspora nearby in North America is large, skilled, and economically supportive.

Moreover, Haiti currently has preferential access to the U.S. market for manufactured goods, especially apparel, Haiti's most important export, through the Haitian Hemispheric Opportunity Through Partnership Encouragement (HOPE) II Act.[1]

Haiti's recent experience has shown that increased social and political stability can create space for economic gains and improvements in the provision of services. Since 2004, the United Nations Stabilization Mission in Haiti (Mission des Nations Unies pour la Stabilisation en Haïti, or MINUSTAH), with 13,000 peacekeepers and police at peak level,[2] has contributed to maintaining security. Improvements in the national police have resulted in better public safety, including declines in gang-related violence and kidnappings. Following the change in government in 2004 came five consecutive years of economic growth. Although the progress achieved in this period was fragile, it indicates that, with renewed effort, Haiti can recover from the effects of the

---

1 Part of Public Law 110-246 (2008).

2 Authorized strength of uniformed personnel in MINUSTAH has risen from 8,322 in April 2004 to 13,331 as of June 2010. See MINUSTAH (undated).

earthquake and embark on a new period of growth and improving public services.

Now that the humanitarian-relief phase of the earthquake response is coming to a close, the Haitian government and foreign donors are considering reconstruction priorities and how to revise Haiti's development plans in light of the earthquake. Haiti and the donor community now need to turn not only to rebuilding infrastructure but also to creating a stronger institutional basis for Haiti's government so that it can improve the provision of justice, security, utilities, education, and health care and gradually diminish its dependence on external support. To accomplish this goal, the Haitian government and international donors would benefit from a careful analysis of realistic options and of how to weave state-building measures throughout reconstruction plans and programs so that Haiti can fortify itself against future calamities.

Not long before the January earthquake, the United Nations (UN) Secretary-General observed, apropos of Haiti, that the "prospects for substantial and lasting improvements in institutional capacity would be greatly enhanced through adoption by the Government of an overall blueprint for State reform, drawing as appropriate upon already existing proposals."[3] In 2007, the government of Haiti had broadly articulated its strategy for pursuing development and economic growth and improving governance in its *Growth and Poverty Reduction Strategy Paper* (GPRSP). A modified form of the GPRSP became the basis for a general strategy for reforming Haiti's economy approved at the April 2009 donors' conference in Washington, D.C.[4] After the earthquake, the government prepared its overarching *Action Plan for National Recovery and Development of Haiti*[5] and a postdisaster needs assessment (PDNA),[6] which it presented at a donors' conference in New York in March 2010.

---

3 UN Security Council (2009b, pp. 14–15).

4 This donors' conference responded to a series of damaging hurricanes and tropical storms in late 2008 and spikes in food and fuel prices. The revised GPRSP is found in Republic of Haiti (2008).

5 Republic of Haiti (2010a).

6 Republic of Haiti (2010b).

These documents provide a broad vision for Haiti's reconstruction and development and identify funding needs. They do not provide a critical examination of preexisting plans in all sectors; nor do they put state-building at the forefront of efforts to ignite progress. In many instances, these plans do not explicitly address the weaknesses of the Haitian state or how those weaknesses might be rectified. They also fail to set realistic goals and priorities. This failure risks squandering resources and, more importantly, the opportunity to set right deeply embedded problems from the past. The Inter-American Development Bank (IDB) notes, in an evaluation of its country program for Haiti, that its own "strategies failed to present a proper diagnosis of the situation beyond a description of some of the many problems. This failure resulted in the inability to effectively prioritize among the different pressing needs that the country faces."[7] This criticism can be extended to most of the existing plans for Haiti's development.

This report is intended to fill this gap by appraising past and current plans to improve the provision of public services in Haiti and providing recommendations on how those plans might be improved. The report focuses on setting priorities for the next few years and suggesting measures that might produce palpable improvements in the provision of public services in Haiti over that period. It is designed to be useful to the government of Haiti as it develops detailed plans for policy and institutional reforms and to the international donor community as it determines how to support the government's efforts.

We prepared this report by conducting our own analysis and engaging collaboratively with representatives of key Haitian and international institutions. We examined all of the principal plan documents relevant to the subject areas we address. We also discussed plans and programs with representatives of the Haitian government, international and multilateral organizations, key bilateral donor agencies, the Haitian private sector, foreign investors, and nonprofit organizations engaged in Haiti. We drew on these discussions to identify pre- and postearthquake state-building and reconstruction challenges, as well as the institutional, economic, and physical obstacles to addressing those

---

7 IDB (2007, p. 15).

challenges. To develop our recommendations, we critically appraised both past proffered solutions and new ones, drawing on the experiences of other societies emerging from conflict and crisis.

Following a brief description in Chapter Two of the overall challenges faced by Haiti, we begin in Chapter Three by focusing on governance and public administration. Throughout the Haitian government, ministries and agencies have long had difficulty implementing policies and delivering public services. The government often struggles to attract and manage the employees it needs. Processes and procedures are often inefficient or burdensome. Important regulations, such as building codes, are frequently outdated or not enforced. If the Haitian government is to greatly improve the quality of services provided in any area, public administration will need to be improved and elected officials will need to perform their roles more effectively.

Subsequently, in Chapters Four and Five, we turn to justice and security. No country can enjoy sustained economic growth or public well-being if violence is endemic and crime goes unchecked. The police force provides the first line of defense. Improvements in the Haitian National Police (HNP) have been notable. Crime has fallen, and public trust has risen. However, the police continue to face many challenges. Assigning priorities and channeling resources to these priorities should lead to continued improvements in this area.

In contrast to the police, little progress has been made in improving the performance of the Haitian judiciary and corrections system. Without more progress in these areas, the newly enlarged and reformed police force could soon deteriorate to its previous level of incompetence and corruption. The Haitian government and the international donor community need to address the problems of carrying out timely and just criminal procedures and resolving disputes more effectively than has been done in the past. They also need to ensure that incarceration is fair and humane.

In Chapter Six, we turn to the challenges of creating an environment for economic growth. We first focus on economic policy, especially the fiscal challenges facing the Haitian government. We also critically comment on the regulatory obstacles the government imposes on businesses. Subsequently, in Chapter Seven, we address the challenges of providing better infrastructure. The Haitian government and the international community have conducted a number of analyses of the roads, ports, and electric-power plants needed to improve transportation and the provision of electricity in Haiti. Our focus is not on needs. Rather, we evaluate the institutional and policy reforms proposed to improve the construction, maintenance, and operation of infrastructure, focusing on measures needed to make the provision of public utilities, such as electric power and water, sustainable.

We then turn to two key services: education (Chapter Eight) and health care (Chapter Nine). Private, nonprofit, and religious institutions are the primary providers of education and health care in Haiti. Despite their efforts, the quality of and access to these services is the worst in the Western Hemisphere. We appraise the role of the Haitian government in providing and regulating these services and suggest ways in which the state could more effectively ensure the delivery of both education and health care.

Finally, in Chapter Ten, we examine current plans for improving coordination of donor activities. We propose ways for donors to engage constructively and collaboratively with the government of Haiti and with each other, to ensure that the postearthquake infusion of donor funds produces the desired effects.

We set common criteria for the recommendations in each of the chapters. The recommendations need to meet the following criteria:

- confined to the most-important priorities
- fiscally sustainable, at least at some not-too-distant point
- commensurate with the administrative capacity of the Haitian government
- realistic in their prospects for implementation within the time frame we set
- geared to enhancing the effectiveness of the Haitian state rather than perpetuating dependence on foreign donors, contractors, and nongovernmental organizations (NGOs)
- coherent, in that the proposed reforms are compatible with each other and directed toward a common goal—the creation of a more capable and resilient Haitian state.

We focus on recommending actions that could commence quickly and that could yield positive outcomes within the next three to five years. We aim for outcomes that will be tangible to Haiti's citizens. Unrealistic plans that do not produce promised results risk disenchantment among the Haitian population and donors, especially legislative bodies responsible for setting donor funding levels. The focus should be on incremental, steady progress.

We hope this report leads to a vigorous discussion and the development of more effective policies and programs for improving conditions in Haiti. Although the earthquake is a tragedy of extraordinary proportions and, in many respects, set back the tentative progress of recent years, it also provides an opportunity to rectify some of the long-term problems besetting the Haitian state and burdening the Haitian people.

CHAPTER TWO

Background

The prototypical fragile state is inaccessible, often land-locked, surrounded by weak or predatory neighbors, and wracked by tribal, ethnic, religious, or linguistic tensions.[1] Haiti suffers from none of these disabilities. It is surrounded by friendly, comparatively prosperous neighbors. It has many natural harbors only a few hours sailing distance from the largest market in the world—the United States—to which it has preferential access.[2] Unlike some fragile states, Haiti has no precious gems, minerals, or other such resources over which parties might fight.

Haiti's fragility cannot be blamed on its geography or its demography, but rather on its history. Treated as a virtual pariah for much of the 19th century by reason of its national origins in a successful slave rebellion, Haiti has, to this day, remained culturally distinct and politically isolated from the Hispanic and Anglophone societies around it. Forced in the 19th century to pay France a massive indemnity for properties lost in that rebellion, Haiti became entrapped in a cycle of poverty and misgovernment from which it has never emerged. In 1915, President Woodrow Wilson authorized a U.S. military intervention that lasted 19 years. The United States left behind a good deal of physical infrastructure, including the recently collapsed presidential palace, but also left behind an abusive Haitian military. From 1957 to 1986,

---

1 On fragile states, see Zoellick (2008); Kaplan (2008a, 2008b); Ghani and Lockhart (2008); Collier (2007); Eizenstat, Porter, and Weinstein (2005); Krasner and Pascual (2005); and Rotberg (2003, 2004).

2 See Collier and Warnholz (2010).

the Duvalier family, first father (François, called Papa Doc) and then son (Jean-Claude, called Baby Doc), ruled—or misruled—Haiti. After a long history of brutal authoritarian rule, Haiti experienced its first real shot at democracy with the election of Jean-Bertrand Aristide in 1990. Reform stalled, however, and support for the democratic movement waned, in part due to Aristide's erratic and populist line. In 1991, a military junta seized power and reinstated governance through repression.[3]

In 1994, after more than three years of internal violence, during which thousands of "boat people" fled Haiti in makeshift boats for the United States, the William J. Clinton administration ejected the junta.[4] President Aristide was returned to power, and relatively fair elections were held in 1995.[5] The United States, politically divided over the intervention, withdrew, leaving behind a democracy with only the shallowest roots.

In the second half of the 1990s, the major powers' attention shifted to the Balkans, while the political situation in Haiti grew increasingly troubled. Aristide was barred from running for office in the 1995 presidential elections but remained a powerful political figure. In the aftermath of those elections, despite the victory of his close ally René Préval, Aristide again took a populist and demagogic line. His broad political movement, Fanmi Lavalas, soon began to fracture.[6] Opposition leaders and supporters of the old regime remained fearful about Haiti's democratic turn. Political violence continued, this time by the democrats against their old repressors, albeit on a smaller scale than in the past.[7]

This political turmoil undermined hope of passing legislation that Haiti needed to stabilize its economy, reform its justice system, and sustain foreign assistance.[8] The situation worsened after the 2000 pres-

---

[3] Fatton (1999; 2002, pp. 77–106).

[4] Morley and McGillion (1997).

[5] Dobbins, McGinn, et al. (2003, p. 79).

[6] Fatton (2002, pp. 112–115).

[7] Dobbins, McGinn, et al. (2003, p. 79).

[8] Buss (2008, pp. 24–26).

idential and parliamentary elections. Aristide and his followers won the elections handily. Allegations of irregularities, however, led to an opposition boycott of the presidential elections, precipitating a political crisis and undermining Aristide's legitimacy and ability to govern.[9]

By 2001, the international community had all but withdrawn from Haiti. Major donors were focused elsewhere, and the UN mission had closed down. Only the Organization of American States (OAS) and Caribbean Community (CARICOM) were still involved on the ground. More than $500 million in international aid was withdrawn, in hopes of bringing recalcitrant parties to the negotiating table. This approach failed, and the only result was more Haitian suffering.[10]

Under these conditions, economic reforms failed to be implemented; economic output fell. The security situation deteriorated as thugs loosely aligned with Haiti's various political forces played a growing role in politics. The renewal of violence was facilitated by Haiti's emergence as a transshipment point for drugs headed from South America to the United States, as well as the endemic weakness of Haiti's state institutions. Poor and lacking military, effective police, or a functioning criminal-justice system, the Haitian state was ill-prepared to maintain law and order or even defend itself against mounting gang violence. Political leaders continued to enrich themselves illegally, to such an extent that, in 2002, the World Bank ranked Haiti the second-most corrupt country in the world.[11]

By early 2004, the Haitian government had effectively lost control of the country. Violence was mounting, and Aristide was under pressure from opposition groups to step down. This time, he received little support from the international community. Faced with the options of self-exile or violent overthrow, he reluctantly accepted U.S. advice to choose the former. Ten years after ousting the military junta, the international community intervened again to stabilize Haiti.[12]

---

[9] Erikson (2005).

[10] Erikson (2005).

[11] Kaufmann, Kraay, and Mastruzzi (2008).

[12] Erikson (2005).

Following the brief deployment of a multilateral force comprised primarily of U.S., Canadian, and French troops, the UN Security Council authorized MINUSTAH at a strength of 6,700 troops. This UN peacekeeping mission was sent in with a mandate to improve the security situation, foster democracy, and support human rights. The Security Council also authorized the deployment of 1,622 civilian police—a significant number. This component signaled recognition not only of Haiti's problems with criminality but also of the fundamental weakness of the Haitian state.[13]

At the start, the going was rough.[14] A transitional government that was, in theory, technocratic in nature continued the divisive politics of the past, including the use of political violence and direct action in the streets through proxies.[15] The UN struggled to control the security situation. In the fall of 2004, gangs still controlled parts of the country. Rioters beheaded three Haitian police officers.[16]

A year after Aristide's departure, the security situation started to improve, although, in July 2005, UN troops were needed to conduct military operations against gang leaders in Port-au-Prince's main slum, Cité Soleil.[17] (These operations continued for the next two years, with positive results.[18]) Elections took place in 2006, and René Préval won the presidency. Subsequently, the security situation remained fragile but stable; key reform legislation was passed; and some efforts to improve public administration, especially financial management, began to gain traction. Economic growth resumed, albeit from an extremely low base, and political stability was improving. Such was the situation when the earthquake struck in January 2010.[19]

---

13 UN Security Council (2004a).

14 See, for example, Caroit (2004).

15 Mobekk (2008); Fatton (2006).

16 UN Security Council (2004b).

17 UN Security Council (2005).

18 Dziedzic and Perito (2008).

19 Buss (2008, pp. 40–44, 169–182).

Haiti's Challenges

Economic Development

Haiti's per capita gross domestic product (GDP) declined by more than one-third in the past 30 years.[20] Haiti also scores low on nearly all other basic development indicators. According to one source, the percentage of the population with access to an improved drinking source in 1989 was 52 percent and had risen to only 58 percent by 2007.[21] A household survey from 2001 found that less than 10 percent of the population had access to potable tap water and that less than one-third had access to electricity, even intermittently.[22] Differences between urban and rural areas, which are, by far, the worst off, are significant. The fact that Haiti's GDP has fallen in several years (see Figure 2.1) is especially

Figure 2.1
Irregular Growth in Haiti's Gross Domestic Product

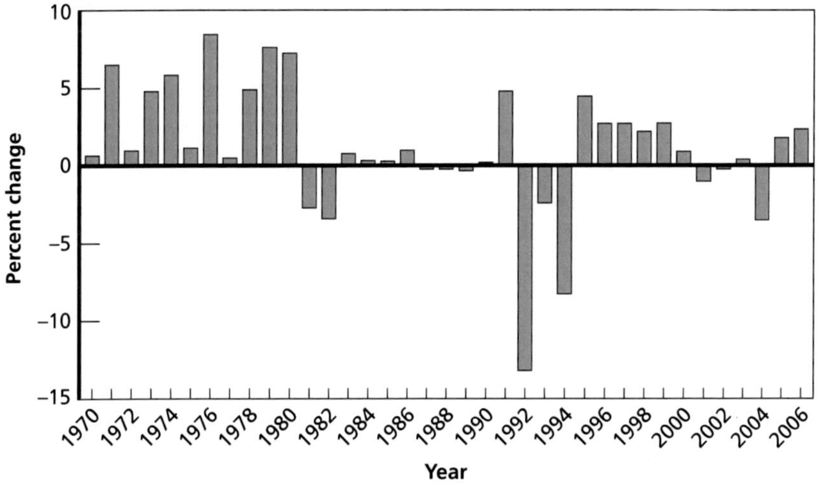

SOURCE: Calculated from IMF (undated).
RAND *MG1039-2.1*

[20] Calculated from IMF (undated): constant per capita income, national currency.

[21] UNSD (undated).

[22] IHSI (2005).

notable given the general correlation between declines in GDP and outbreaks of violence and civil war.[23]

More than half of Haiti's population lives on less than $1 per day. More than three-quarters live on less than $2 per day. Haiti's exports are small: only 10 percent of GDP. Remittances are important, constituting some 9 percent of GDP.[24] Remittances are an indicator of the strength of Haiti's large expatriate community in Canada and the United States—a community that, in theory at least, could also be a source of expertise and human capital.[25]

Haiti's poor economic performance is, in part, the result of the decline of its agricultural sector. Environmental degradation is both cause and consequence of this decline. According to Yale University, Haiti ranks 155th out of 163 countries when it comes to general environmental degradation, while the neighboring Dominican Republic ranks 36th.[26] Less than 3 percent of Haiti is covered by forest, creating a "moonscape" that disappears when one travels across the border into the lush forests of the Dominican Republic.[27]

While Haiti's economic problems obviously have economic and natural causes—lack of investment capital, lack of skilled labor, and the devastation caused by hurricanes and earthquakes, to name a few—it would be too simplistic to confine explanations of Haiti's impoverishment to these factors. Social and political problems also affect Haiti's poor economic performance. So, too, does Haiti's poor economic performance contribute to its political and social problems. Poverty, in particular, increases the volatility of Haitian politics, is a root cause of Haiti's social underdevelopment, and, through its fiscal effects, weakens the institutional apparatus of the Haitian state. Economic weakness also contributes to corruption, enlarges the pool of

---

23 See Miguel, Satyanath, and Sergenti (2004).

24 IMF (2009a).

25 This point is often noted. See, for example, Wente (2010).

26 Rankings available from EPI (undated).

27 Dolisca et al. (2007); Kristof (2010).

potential recruits for gang violence, and enhances the attractiveness of the drug trade.

Society

The vast majority of the rural population is severely impoverished, and hunger is widespread. Children in remote parts of Haiti sometimes die from malnutrition.[28] Although infant mortality dropped from 152 per 1,000 in 1989 to 76 per 1,000 in 2007, Haiti still ranks 46th from the bottom in global rankings, in a range with Yemen, Pakistan, and India. This is a slight improvement since 1989, when it ranked 30th worst.[29]

Although informal social networks can be strong and influential in Haiti, conventional civil society of the kind found in developed democracies is weak there. The repressiveness of the Duvalier regime and chaos of the past two decades has not been conducive to widespread participation in politics and civic groups.[30]

Fortunately, Haiti is not divided along ethnic or tribal lines. However, Haitian society is highly stratified, with a small economic elite and a large number of very poor.[31] Despite the fall in per capita GDP during the past several decades, a small number of Haitians live relatively well; in 2001, almost half the country's income went to the wealthiest 10 percent of society.[32] Income inequality is among the widest in the world.[33] The lack of a middle class is a problem not only because it weakens the economy but also because the middle class could provide a much-needed source of talent for government bureaucracies and businesses. Income inequality results in very different interests among the different classes. Because of these different interests, these groups often have difficulty finding common ground.

---

[28] Taft-Morales (2009).

[29] UNSD (undated).

[30] See Putnam (1993).

[31] Mintz (1995); Malone (2004).

[32] World Bank (undated [c], p. 66).

[33] UNDP (2009).

State Administration

Historically, the Haitian state has served as an apparatus by which elites extract rents from the impoverished population, not as a means of serving Haiti's citizens.[34] Corruption is a serious problem; Haiti ranked 168 of 180 in Transparency International's *Corruption Perceptions Index* in 2008, in the same league as Iran and Turkmenistan. Since 2002, when it was first included in the rankings, it has slipped slightly, from the 87th percentile to the 93rd.[35] Haiti also ranks very low on broader governance indicators; Figure 2.2 shows the evolution of Haiti's governance rankings over the past 15 years.

A weak economy and low levels of social development impede the development of effective state administration. A narrow tax base, weak fiscal capacity, and corruption deprive the state of revenues.[36]

Figure 2.2
Haiti's Persistently Low Ranking on Governance

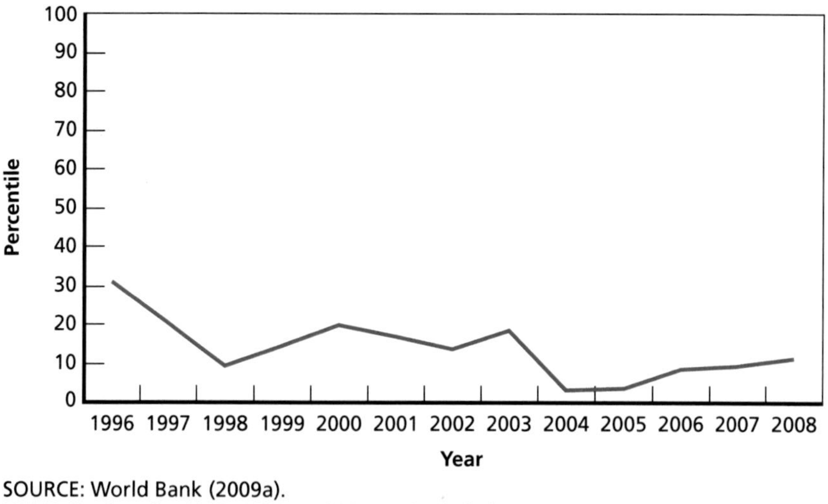

SOURCE: World Bank (2009a).
NOTE: No data for 1997, 1999, or 2001 are included.
RAND *MG1039-2.2*

---

[34] Fatton (2002).

[35] Calculated from figures available from Transparency International (2009).

[36] Allix (2010).

Low levels of social development result in low levels of human capital available for employment in the state administration.

A history of dictatorial rule has resulted in widespread suspicion of state security forces. Aristide disbanded the military after his return to power in 1994, and efforts to build an effective police force have, until very recently, been largely unsuccessful. Without effective security forces and judicial and penal systems, the Haitian state has been unable to establish public order and the rule of law, and the government's legitimacy has suffered as a result.

For their part, international donors have often been unwilling to invest in state institutions, perpetuating their weakness. Corruption, political turmoil, and a general lack of capacity encourage international donors to channel funds through NGOs instead. As a result, the Haitian state is significantly weaker than it could be, and dependence on foreign donors is reinforced.

Politics

The Haitian government's incapacity to deal with hurricanes, earthquakes, and domestic conflict is not just a function of the country's poverty and will not be corrected just with added resources, no matter how lavishly and wisely applied. Indeed, Haiti's poverty, like its governmental weakness, is a product of its political culture. Thus, any effort to build a stronger, more-resilient Haiti, one that is less dependent on external help, will depend on changing that culture.

Haiti's failure to develop is often blamed on resistance from a small, wealthy elite to changes that might threaten their position. This is a considerable oversimplification. In fact, resistance to change is manifest across the political spectrum from entrenched rent-seeking interest groups fearful of losing their slices of a very small pie. Henry Kissinger once jokingly attributed the severity of academic disputes to the limited nature of the stakes. Haiti offers a more serious example of this phenomenon. Modernizing the port of Port-au-Prince, for example, is resisted because it might reduce employment. Privatizing the electric company is resisted because people, particularly poorer people, might have to pay for what little electricity they get. It was the radical populist President Aristide who ultimately turned away from the market-oriented economic reforms he had promised on his return to power in 1994, and it has been forces associated with him, and thus with Haiti's poorest citizens, that have resisted many reforms since.

Haiti's democratic transition has been contested, and its politics remain fractious. Since 1980, Haiti has experienced a coup, two international military interventions, a democratic implosion, a period of "technocratic" tutelage, and a return to democracy characterized by ongoing political gridlock and instability. In all but the most recent years, Haitian politics have been cacophonous and thuggish. This history adversely affects the expectations and outlook of Haiti's political elites and citizens alike.

Despite recent improvements, it is too soon to assume that democracy has fully taken root. The problem is, in part, constitutional—there are serious questions about whether the French-modeled constitution introduced after the fall of the Duvalier regime is really the best for Haiti—but the problem, in many ways, goes deeper. In order for democracy to work, a process in which "democratic norms come to be valued in themselves, even against adverse substantive outcomes" needs to unfold.[37]

This kind of change is possible, but it almost never happens overnight. On the most basic level, for Haiti to develop a stable, representative government, the country's political forces must fully accept the legitimacy of the democratic process, even if it is not in their immediate interest. This is true both for the forces of the old regime and for the forces that support democracy.

Often, this acceptance involves some agreement or "pact" among elites on the fundamental limits and rules of government, as well as some mechanism to ensure that these rules are enforced so that Haiti's political groups can have confidence that others will abide by them.[38] In fragile states, this is often one of the most difficult challenges, given the disincentives for elites to cooperate.[39] Once achieved, however, the

---

37 Weingast (1997). See also Almond and Verba (1963) and Przeworski (1991).

38 Weingast (1997).

39 Kaplan (2008a).

practice of democratic politics encourages democratic legitimization and the deepening of democratic culture.

In Haiti, several factors have impeded this process, including the following:

- The fractiousness of the political system hampers the development of elite consensus about the rules of the game. Ongoing wrangling over reforms to and interpretation of the Haitian constitution is a case in point.[40]
- The wide disparity in income in the context of widespread poverty means that the old regime has much to lose from redistribution and, hence, little interest in compromise.
- The politically motivated violence of the recent past increases the stakes and risks of compromise, thereby reducing overall trust.
- The weakness of Haiti's political parties contributes to the general fractiousness of the system.
- Venality in all branches of government undermines the rule of law and perpetuates a culture of rent-seeking.

As a consequence of the fragility of Haitian democracy, policymaking is extremely difficult. Any strategy designed to improve the effectiveness of the Haitian state must recognize that, despite positive signs prior to the earthquake, Haiti has not yet consolidated its democracy. Were the Haitian government to collapse again, the international investment could evaporate once more.

Consequences of the Earthquake

According to the Haitian government, 300,000 people died in the earthquake.[41] Estimates of the physical damage run from $7 billion to $14 billion.[42] The effects on economic growth and social progress are

---

40 On the adequacies of the 1987 constitution, see Gros (1997).

41 See Republic of Haiti (2010a, p. 7).

42 Cavallo, Powell, and Becerra (2010). See also Taft-Morales and Margesson (2010).

great. The physical destruction precipitated a humanitarian catastrophe and has resulted in a severe decline in economic activity and an extraordinary disruption of society, politics, and the state administration. The destruction of infrastructure exacerbated existing economic problems and reduced the quality of life of all Haitians. The collapse of buildings and the partial destruction of the port of Port-au-Prince are complicating efforts to revive foreign trade. The destruction of some 30,000 commercial buildings has increased the unemployment rate, while the loss of 180 government buildings has hindered the operations of an already ineffective state; surviving ministers and civil servants have been forced to work from makeshift premises, sometimes outdoors.[43]

After the earthquake, about 60 percent of the prison population, including several hundred hardened criminals, escaped. While the security situation has been kept under control, in large part due to the presence of international forces, escapees—particularly gang leaders and members arrested in the 2007 crackdown—pose a threat to security.[44]

Haiti and Donors

For most of the 1990s, the Haitian government was at odds with foreign donors. In 2002, the World Bank's Operations Evaluation Department noted that it was "all but impossible to carry on a coherent lending program."[45] Donors, including the U.S. Agency for International Development (USAID), stopped and restarted development assistance to Haiti several times, as political responses to coups and abuses of power by Haitian authorities, as well as due to differences over economic policies (Figure 2.3).

In the 1996–2000 period, major donors sought to encourage the development of civil society, privatize state-owned enterprises,

---

43 International Crisis Group (2010).

44 DPKO (undated); International Crisis Group (2010, p. 10).

45 World Bank (2002, p. 17).

Figure 2.3
Ups and Downs of Assistance to Haiti, All Donors

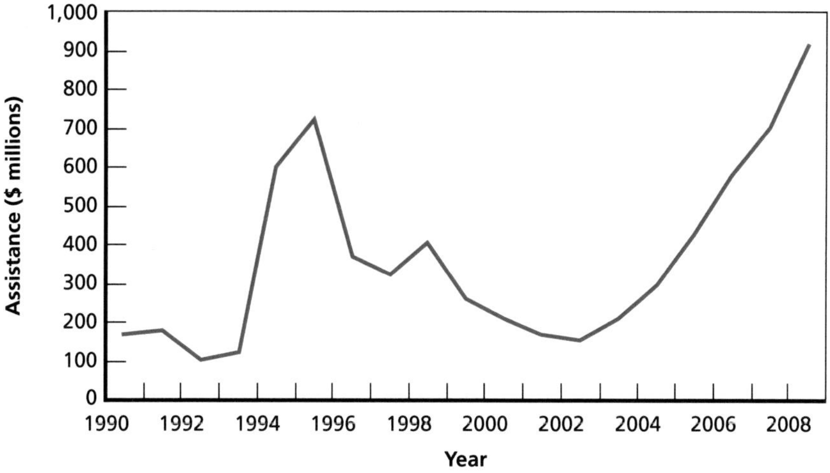

SOURCE: OECD (undated [b]).
RAND *MG1039-2.3*

and decentralize the state, but the Haitian government considered all three of these initiatives threats to its power and authority, despite its recognition of the need for external funding. Donor initiatives were stymied by passive resistance by ministries and opposition in Haiti's parliament. The World Bank, mandated to work through government institutions, eventually closed its office in Haiti and halted new commitments. Bilateral donors responded by increasing the use of Haitian and international NGOs to deliver services, including health care, sanitation and education, further aggravating the responsibility deficit, as well as the Haitian government's capacity shortfalls.

After the events of 2004, however, cooperation between the Haitian government, donors, and NGOs improved significantly. A first post-Aristide meeting of donors, international agencies, and the government was held in Port-au-Prince in late April 2004. A donor team representing the United Nations, the World Bank, the IDB, and the European Commission followed up by hosting a two-day workshop with transitional-government ministers and representatives of Haitian civil society to craft a two-year plan to restart the economy and improve social services. The workshop (and three meetings held in provincial towns the following week) kicked off a one-and-a-half-month effort by officials, experts, and donors (including representatives of 26 bilateral, multilateral, and UN agencies working in ten "thematic groups") to define a development strategy. The workshop emphasized the importance of ownership by the government of Haiti and was the first joint strategy development effort of its kind.

The result was the Cadre de Coopération Intérimaire or Interim Cooperation Framework (ICF), which the Haitian government presented to a donors' conference in Washington in July 2004. The ICF was intended to identify "quick wins." It established a two-year framework for assistance programs that sought to align goals and resources. It specified needs of $1.37 billion over the period and catalogued $127 million in available national budget resources and $315 million in previous donor pledges. This meant a two-year financing gap of $924 million, which was covered by pledges at the July donors' conference. A new donors' cooperation process also was created, led by the World Bank. The ICF anticipated the subsequent preparation of a more comprehensive framework document, the GPRSP.[46]

The World Bank adopted its own two-year transitional support strategy based on the ICF, emphasizing "community-driven" development aimed at helping Haiti meet basic, urgent needs, deliver income-generating opportunities, and strengthen economic governance. Under this strategy, the World Bank (as well as the IDB and other donors) supported a program to improve the management of public finances.[47] Meanwhile, a core donor group was created in Washington.

The effort at cooperation between the Haitian government and donors was unprecedented, but implementation of the ambitious program was slow. By March 2005, only $220 million had been disbursed

46 Republic of Haiti (2004).

47 Discussion with Ministry of Economy and Finance official, Port-au-Prince, April 19, 2010. The program includes adoption of United Nations Conference on Trade and Development (UNCTAD) systems for managing trade data and customs receipts, and the SYSDEP system management of government expenditures.

of the $924 million in new funds pledged.[48] With the exception of support for elections, for which the United Nations Development Programme (UNDP) managed a mechanism for pooling contributions, there was no trust fund–like mechanism. Most donors continued to undertake projects directly by subcontracting to NGOs and implementing partners. With World Bank support, a coordination cell was established in the prime minister's office to track ICF implementation. Even so, a UNDP "lessons learned" paper concluded that the Haitian government and the donor community had difficulties consistently tracking disbursements of pledges and that reports to subsequent donors' conferences were "unverifiable and appeared to be based on guesswork."[49]

Following the election of President René Préval in 2006, the formulation of the GPRSP began. It was completed following a yearlong process of domestic consultation and substantial donor involvement and advice. The government of Haiti adopted the resulting document in November 2007.[50] It had been a condition of Haiti's debt-reduction agreement with the International Monetary Fund (IMF) that the GPRSP be in place for one year before debt reduction was granted.[51]

The document laid out a strategy agreed among the Haitian government and the donor and NGO communities, although outside analysts criticized it as lacking clear priorities and operational details.[52] For the first time, the GPRSP included a section on monitoring and evaluation,[53] tasking the Ministry of Planning and External Cooperation (Ministère de la Planification et de la Coopération Externe) with this responsibility. A national office for implementation coordination, with subordinate directorates for research, public investment, external

[48] UNDG (2006, p. 11).

[49] UNDG (2006, pp. 13–14).

[50] The IMF has made an unofficial English translation of the French original available (IMF, 2008).

[51] Call (2009, fn. 31).

[52] Call (2009, p. 10).

[53] Republic of Haiti (2008, fn. 9, ¶¶251–261).

cooperation, and NGO-activity coordination, looked impressive in design but, in fact, had limited capacity to track development activities systematically.[54] In response to the GPRSP, bilateral donors, such as the United States, increased assistance to Haiti but, in most cases, used the existing network of NGOs to deliver services.

In 2008, Haiti was battered by four hurricanes and tropical storms. In part to help Haiti generate employment opportunities following these disasters, the U.S. Congress, with bipartisan support, passed the HOPE II Act. This law allows apparel factories in Haiti to utilize third country–sourced fabric to produce substantial quantities of apparel for duty-free access into the United States under the Caribbean Basin Trade Partnership Act.[55] In designing HOPE II, the U.S. Congress sought to ensure that workers' rights be protected. Consequently, the U.S. Congress mandated that Better Work, a program managed by the International Labour Organization and the International Finance Corporation, set up a Haitian technical-assistance program.[56] Hanesbrands, Gildan Activewear, and other apparel firms opened or expanded Haitian operations in response to the trade-preference opportunity; exports to the U.S. market rose quickly.[57]

In response to these natural disasters, donors also worked together with the Haitian government to develop a shorter, more prioritized development plan, which again accorded the Haitian government the lead for direction and strategy. The plan, *Haiti: A New Paradigm*,[58] sought to create 100,000–150,000 jobs in two years, in part by taking advantage of new U.S. and other trade-preference opportunities and

---

[54] Discussion with Ministry of Economy and Finance official, April 2010.

[55] Public Law 106-200 (2000).

[56] Nathan Associates (2009). As of May 2010, on the basis of a request from former Presidents Bill Clinton and George W. Bush, congressional committees were considering tripling quantitative limits and extending the program by two years, to 2020.

[57] U.S. imports of knit and nonknit apparel increased 24.4 percent in 2009 over the previous year and by 19.2 percent over the average of the previous four years (RAND calculations based on U.S. Department of Commerce data obtained from International Trade Administration, undated).

[58] *Haiti: A New Paradigm* (2009).

in part through the reconstruction of infrastructure following the storms. The plan was presented at a donors' conference in April 2009, aimed in large part at securing pledges of budget support to cover an estimated Haitian government budget gap of $175 million. Pledges of $324 million in new funding were made, fully covering the request for budget support. In the process, the United States pledged $20 million for budget support—the first time it had done so for Haiti.[59] To support the new plan, donors also established a joint committee with the government of Haiti to monitor the implementation of measures to enhance the transparency of the budget process, strengthen the government's capacity to account to Parliament, and track the disbursements of pledged assistance.[60]

Following the conference, the U.S. government, the largest bilateral donor, began a comprehensive interagency review of its strategy for Haiti with the objective of increasing aid effectiveness and focus. The intention was for the United States to lead the way for similar strategy reviews by other bilateral donors. The review found that overall U.S. assistance was large but that programs were so varied and were individually so small as to limit their impact. The review proposed that the United States focus on priority sectors in which assistance could have the greatest impact and end support for programs in some other areas. The new U.S. strategy was developed and briefed for approval at a National Security Council Deputies Committee meeting on January 12, 2010, only hours before the earthquake hit.[61]

---

59 Varma (2009).

60 *Haiti: A New Paradigm* (2009, p. 6).

61 Discussion with U.S. State Department official, March 25, 2010.

CHAPTER THREE

Governance and Public Administration

Reforming public administration is at the heart of state-building in Haiti. The paucity of skilled, trained, and properly organized government personnel and the lack of management systems within ministries and other government bodies are principal constraints on the state's effectiveness. The implications of the institutional deficiencies in planning, budgeting, executing policy decisions, and managing people and resources cut across all the areas of government activity covered in this report, including the government's ability to interact with donors.

Capacity-building is often invoked as the answer to the state's weakness; this chapter aims to give content to that generic and overused term. The Haitian state needs the *capacity* to plan and carry out policies, ensure the delivery of services to the public (whether or not it actually delivers the services itself), and set, monitor, and enforce standards. *Building* that capacity requires putting in place the right people, structures, and procedures.

Building a capable public bureaucracy is part of Haiti's broader challenge of transitioning from being a place where leadership and governance are personal to one in which the law-bound structures and procedures of the state have permanence and legitimacy. This transition will not occur quickly, but much work can begin now to strengthen and fill gaps in state institutions and to improve democratic governance.

With some exceptions, government plans to improve public administration have not attracted significant donor support—even while donors lament the government's inability to work as an effective partner. Donors will need to support these plans if the Haitian government is to become more effective, a prerequisite for successful reconstruction and development in Haiti.

The Challenges

Long-Standing Challenges

Governance. The quality of democratic governance—that is, the performance of the political system generally and elected officials particularly—has a major impact on how well state institutions function and on the prospects for adopting state-building reforms. Haiti has a long history of predatory government and a more recent history of nearly absent government. Small elites of both left and right have long dominated politics, and there is little in the way of an organized political-party system. Hiring based on political patronage is endemic and deeply affects competence and accountability in public administration. For the most part, these fundamental political issues cannot be resolved through technical measures; rather, leadership on the part of Haitian officials and a combination of pressure applied and incentives offered by donors will be needed to overcome the political obstacles to state-building.

Parliament's institutional weakness—despite its political power—has especially hampered state-building.[1] Parliament is ill-equipped to perform its legislative and oversight functions effectively, impeding adoption of many laws needed to improve the legal framework for public administration and address other issues of public concern. Many of the recommendations throughout this report will require legal changes, but, until now, Parliament has been slow to pass important legislation. This includes budget laws, which are regularly delayed; the 2008–2009 budget law, for example, was adopted eight months into the fiscal year.[2] About one-third to one-half of scheduled parliamentary sessions fail to take place for lack of a quorum.[3] Many parliamentar-

---

1 Call (2009, p. 7).

2 UN Security Council (2009b, p. 2).

3 Discussion with foreign diplomat, Port-au-Prince, April 19, 2010.

ians are inexperienced and poorly regarded; for a significant number, being a member of Parliament is their first job.[4] Turnover at elections at 90–95 percent is exceedingly high.[5] Parliament often operates as a patronage machine, in which the members see their roles as being "development agents" who secure funding for local projects.[6]

The Constitution. Haiti's 1987 constitution is widely regarded as an impediment to effective governance and public administration. Many of its provisions react to the abuses of the Duvalier period—for example, by giving the parliament significant power and the executive few countervailing authorities.[7] Ministry organizational reforms must be effected through legislation. The constitution calls for an extraordinary amount of implementing legislation, much of which has not been adopted.[8] It requires frequent elections, which Haiti can ill afford and which tend to produce periods of instability. And it contains provisions that impede reform in specific areas, such as the justice system, which is saddled, for example, with a constitutionally embedded investigating magistrate structure that poorly serves the Haitian public.

The constitutional-amendment procedure is complex and requires supermajorities at all stages. Parliament must first adopt—in the last regular session of a legislative period—a declaration that the constitution should be amended. Then, in the first session of the next legislative period, it must decide on the proposed amendments. After that, any approved amendments may take effect only after the installation of the next elected president.[9] Shortly before going out of session in the spring of 2010, the Haitian parliament adopted a declaration that the constitution should be amended, but the content of possible amendments has not yet been agreed, and some that have been under discussion (such

---

[4] Discussion with international organization representative, Washington, D.C., March 18, 2010.

[5] Discussion with foreign diplomat, Port-au-Prince, April 19, 2010.

[6] Discussion with representative of Haitian NGO, Port-au-Prince, April 23, 2010.

[7] Gros (1997, pp. 99–100).

[8] Implementing legislation is mentioned 107 times, according to one Haitian legal expert whom we consulted.

[9] Constitution of the Republic of Haiti, 1987, Title XIII.

as an extension of the presidential term limit and reconstitution of the military) are controversial.

Decentralization and Deconcentration. Decentralizing government, and deconcentrating it—that is, moving some responsibility for public administrative services out of Port-au-Prince—have been on the reform agenda since the end of the Duvalier period. However, the physical apparatus of government, decisionmaking, and resources remain highly centralized and concentrated. In reaction to the Duvalier regime's tight hold on and abuse of power, the 1987 constitution prescribes a three-tiered structure of local and regional government, although it does not clearly spell out which responsibilities are to be assigned to the different levels.[10] Each territorial level (communal section, commune, and department) is supposed to have an elected council and an assembly; the constitution calls for an interdepartmental assembly as well. In the December 2006 local elections, 29,000 candidates vied for 1,429 offices.[11]

This complex system has never been fully implemented or funded. Legislation is needed to spell out how authorities and resources are to be distributed among the various levels.[12] Administrative capacity at the local level remains "extremely limited,"[13] posing a major obstacle to decentralization. Some observers consider the main obstacle to decentralization and deconcentration, however, to be politics: Neither Parliament nor government officials located in Port-au-Prince are interested in devolving any of their power or resources.[14]

The government's *Programme-Cadre de Réforme de l'Etat*, to which we refer as the *framework program*,[15] states that the precondi-

---

[10] World Bank (2006, p. 42).

[11] Perito and Jocic (2008, p. 2).

[12] A law was drafted but not sent to Parliament for action in 2008. The draft law would have transferred some tax revenue to the commune and communal-section levels.

[13] UN Security Council (2009b, p. 5).

[14] Email communication with international organization representative, May 19, 2010; discussion with different international organization representative, Washington, D.C., March 18, 2010.

[15] Republic of Haiti (2007).

tions for decentralization have not yet been fulfilled, although the process should be launched. It highlights, among a long list of objections, the missing legal framework, limited resources for local authorities, low administrative and technical capacity in local governments, and lack of consensus on issues of decentralization.

Deconcentration of central government services is meant to address the very uneven availability of administrative services around the country. The concept has not yet been fully elaborated in a national policy or in plans for implementation. In light of Haiti's limited human and financial resources, extending the presence of the government throughout the country will be a challenge.

Human Resources. "Brain drain" is a major problem in Haiti. Many skilled professionals have left the country. University graduates look for work abroad. Low wages and poor working conditions have made it difficult for the civil service to attract those qualified individuals who have remained in Haiti. The capabilities of personnel below the most senior levels of the ministries are usually weak; in particular, there are too few people qualified to work in middle-management positions, while ministries have too many low-level staff.[16] As a consequence, virtually all government decisions are made by a small number of people.

The civil service is disorganized. The government's framework program[17] identifies the need to develop merit-based competition for employment, job descriptions and classifications, a salary scale, a performance-evaluation system, and a manpower plan based on actual needs rather than the discretion of ministry officials. The law on public administration permits public employees to be dismissed, but no procedures are in place for actually doing so.[18] Patronage and lack of accountability are manifest in the large number of "phantom" employees—by one report, about 30 percent of the payroll goes to nonexistent government employees.[19] Absenteeism is common. According

[16] Discussion with Haitian government official, Port-au-Prince, April 21, 2010.

[17] Republic of Haiti (2007).

[18] Discussion with Haitian government official, Port-au-Prince, April 21, 2010.

[19] See Buss (2006, p. 12).

to one estimate, about two-thirds of civil servants also have jobs in NGOs.[20]

Civil service reform has moved slowly. The Office of Human Resources Management (Office de Management et des Ressources Humaines, or OMRH), under the prime minister's office, was set up in 2007 but is still in the early stages of institutionalizing its operations. Some preparatory steps toward improved management, such as carrying out a census of civil servants, have reportedly been completed,[21] though some experts indicate that a clear sense of who is in the civil service and what they are supposed to be doing is still missing.

Public Financial Management and Procurement. Haiti has long had dysfunctional budgetary, financial, and procurement systems. From 1997 to 2001, there was no approved national budget. Auditing has been weak to nonexistent. Procurement has been in the hands of individual ministries; financial controls on them have been weak. Government contracting has been an avenue for corruption.[22] A 2002 World Bank report found "[s]erious weaknesses in financial management practices," including poor recordkeeping, misuse of funds, and noncompetitive bidding procedures.[23]

Since 2004, international financial institutions have put significant effort into helping the central government improve public financial management and procurement, focusing on the Ministry of Economy and Finance (Ministère de l'Economie et des Finances). This effort appears to be paying off: Public financial management is one area that has begun to show improvement. For example, by 2006, ministries' use of their own current accounts—which make it possible for them to spend outside regular budget procedures—was reduced from more than 63 percent of spending in 2004 to less than 10 percent.[24]

---

[20] Discussion with academic expert, Washington, D.C., February 25, 2010.

[21] IDB (2008, p. 8).

[22] See Buss (2006, p. 11).

[23] World Bank (2002, p. 4).

[24] IDB (2008, p. 4; 2007, p. 33). The latter document notes, however, that "it is not clear what the impacts of that reduction have been in terms of quality of public spending."

In addition, important ground has been laid for better administration through adoption of an automated system for budget management (SYSDEP), improved public accounting and procurement systems,[25] and the establishment of an anticorruption unit.[26] In June 2009, Parliament adopted a new law on public procurement—a condition for forgiveness of a significant part of Haiti's external debt.[27] An asset-declaration law and a debt-management system have been put in place as well. While progress in establishing a sound framework for public-finance management has been made, actual implementation and enforcement of the formal rules are still in the early stages.[28]

Consequences of the Earthquake

The earthquake's effect on the logistical aspects of government operations was severe. Many civil servants died; survivors have been traumatized; some government officials were trapped and injured in their own offices. The seats of all three branches of government were destroyed, and many other facilities besides, including the prime minister's office, almost all ministry headquarters, and 180 other government buildings.[29] Files, archives, office equipment, and computer data were also lost. Government officials were dispersed to temporary locations around the capital.

Following the earthquake, there is a high risk that physical reconstruction needs related to restoring government operations will draw funds away from public-administration improvement projects. The government has indicated that reconstruction of its buildings is at the

---

[25] This includes the establishment, in 2004, of the Commission Nationale des Marchés Publics, which has assumed responsibility for procurement (over a specified threshold) previously held by ministries individually.

[26] L'Unité de Lutte Contre la Corruption.

[27] UN Security Council (2009b, p. 2).

[28] Discussion with international organization representative, Washington, D.C., April 5, 2010.

[29] International Crisis Group (2010, p. 2). The report states that 13 of 15 ministries were destroyed; in discussions with the research team, others cited slightly higher figures (for both the number of ministries and the number destroyed).

top of its agenda, and, for example, has asked the IDB to shift funds from support for the OMRH to rebuilding infrastructure.

Demand on the public administration's limited capacity for planning and management may increase as a result of the earthquake in light of the role it is expected to play in overseeing reconstruction. The huge increase in multilateral and bilateral donor funding in response to the earthquake will heighten demand for government interaction with donors and participation in coordination mechanisms. Meetings with visiting donor-agency officials alone will stretch the government's thin human resources.

Scheduled parliamentary and presidential elections were postponed in the aftermath of the earthquake. Reconstruction is thus being launched in a period of uncertainty as to the shape of the next government and questions concerning the government's scope of authority in the absence of an operating parliament. Moreover, the potential for political turmoil when elections are eventually held cannot be discounted.

Appraisal of Plans and Initiatives for Addressing the Challenges

Plans and Initiatives Before the Earthquake

GPRSP. The GPRSP briefly addresses "state capacity-building." It identifies three main themes for state reform: developing human resources, implementing managerial reform, and modernizing administrative technology and the physical work environment. It lists six "major reform programs" in relation to those themes: introduction of a new civil service system; modernization of the central administration's management systems; deconcentration of public services; launching of the decentralization process; modernization of the physical work environment for public services; and technological modernization of public administration.

Each of the six program areas is elaborated by a list of "objectives," which are more in the nature of tasks. For example, under civil service reform, one item is preparation of a recruitment policy, and, under decentralization, one item is preparation of a comprehensive decentralization policy. The GPRSP does not order these tasks in terms of priority or the sequence in which they should be implemented, nor does it provide timelines. It does not provide benchmarks or assign responsibilities for action. As a result, it serves as a statement of anticipated reform actions, but not as a strategy.

Programme-Cadre de Réforme de l'Etat. The framework program—drafted by a group of academics from the diaspora—builds on the same six program areas as the GPRSP but is significantly longer and more detailed. The framework program breaks down the six areas into 32 components; the components are further divided into a total of 249 subcomponents, some of which individually are substantial tasks. Subcomponents include such activities as drafting laws, preparing analyses and conducting studies, and elaborating policy statements. While some subcomponents are concrete (e.g., inventory and appraisal of movable and immovable property of the state), others are vague (e.g., investigate practices and procedures existing in public administration). An annex provides costs per year for each subcomponent, although it does not explain the costing methodology. In terms of anticipated actions, the framework program is very ambitious; the total cost that the document projects for all those actions is under $40 million.

The document identifies periods of execution in one-year increments for the activities listed but, despite its length, does not set priorities or assign responsibilities for action. To a limited extent, it suggests a sequence of actions by linking each subcomponent to a particular year or years, but the logic of the sequencing is, at times, unclear. For example, a study concerning establishment of a system of evaluation for civil servants is scheduled for the same two years in which the government is to elaborate an order creating a system of evaluation. More logically, a study should be completed before creating a system based on its results. Similarly, a study on job descriptions and classifications is scheduled for two years, and an order specifying job classifications is to be elaborated during the second year of the study. It may be that the timelines were loosely drafted or that contradictions in sequencing resulted from squeezing too much work into a five-year time frame.

The framework program helpfully emphasizes the need to collect information and data on which to base policy decisions—in other words, diagnostic work. It also identifies gaps in the legal framework. Overall, it sets out a comprehensive picture of what needs to be done to "modernize" public administration in the areas it covers (it does not address public finance, procurement, or anticorruption) and to work toward decentralization. However, it is overly ambitious for a five-year period. The lack of discussion of who will carry out all the anticipated activities is a major gap. It is more useful as a detailed expression of policy options than a prescription for action.

As the Haitian government was not able to secure full donor funding to implement the framework program, it adopted a gradual approach to implementation as funds became available. For example, Canada funded work on job classification, a salary scale, and recruitment procedures. The IDB worked on public procurement and asset declaration. UNDP provided funds for a few small studies. The World Bank supported the development of a pilot database system for managing human resources. None of these initiatives involved very large sums: The World Bank contributed $150,000 for the database project, for example; projects costing $170,000 had been scheduled to be launched at the time of the earthquake. The most significant funding was $10 million from the IDB for a variety of projects, including an inventory of five ministries' assets.[30] The scope and lack of prioritization in the plan allowed donors to pick and choose which activities they wished to support, making the funded projects unlikely to result in a coherent program.

Revised Plans

Following the earthquake, the Haitian government and donors stated that they would focus on improving public administration in the course of reconstruction. They acknowledged that the weaknesses of the Haitian state—for example, lax or no regulation and enforcement of construction standards, lack of urban planning, and the absence of an emergency response system—contributed greatly to the scale of the

---

[30] Discussion with Haitian government official, Port-au-Prince, April 21, 2010.

disaster. These gaps are intimately related to the state's lack of capacity to fulfill ordinary government functions. So far, however, the post-earthquake exhortations to build the capacity of the state have not been translated into a strategic plan.

Action Plan and PDNA. The government's PDNA and its *Action Plan for National Recovery and Development*[31]—prepared under great time pressure—both treat governance and public-administration issues only briefly, though they differ in important respects in what they say on these subjects. Either document would require considerable elaboration to serve as the basis for a strategic plan. They contain an assortment of reform ideas and tasks but do not assign responsibilities for action. There is no readily discernible logic for their costing.

The PDNA calls for $75 million over three years for reconstruction in the area of "democratic process," though it does not identify on what this money would be spent. It also indicates a need for $387 million over three years for a minimally specified set of activities to bolster public administration, including restructuring ministries, reinforcing human capabilities, possible salary enhancements "to fight against brain drain," movement toward power-sharing with local authorities, and wide-scale computerization. It calls for an additional $407 million over three years for deconcentration and decentralization. The latter two figures combined are about 20 times more (for three years) than the identified cost of the much more extensive framework program (for five years), even though construction of buildings to house government offices is not mentioned in connection with the higher figures. The cost estimates for one or the other (or both) of these plans must be inaccurate, but it is difficult to discern which, given the lack of explanation for the figures. Preparation of a realistic, feasible reform plan will have to be more rigorous in terms of costing.

The action plan sets out different tasks and costs from those in the PDNA, under the rubric of "institutional restructuring." It calls for support for Parliament ($20 million) and for institutions, such as the Electoral Council and Office of National Identification ($75 million), as well as $60 million for elections. For the central public administra-

---

[31] Republic of Haiti (2010a).

tion, it emphasizes constructing buildings, providing temporary premises, and supplying equipment, with priority for the president's and prime minister's offices and eight ministries.

The action plan emphasizes decentralization and deconcentration. It says that a program will be set up to provide incentives for government workers to accept postings outside of Port-au-Prince and sets numerical targets for deconcentration: 80 percent of services (*not* including police, teachers, and health service staff) deconcentrated within five years and 50 percent of the population receiving basic services from their municipality within five years. No analysis is provided to support these targets. The action plan also calls for a training plan and a program for involving the diaspora in public service. In addition, the action plan states that implementing the framework program should be continued, after making adjustments. Under the action plan, costs for central public administration and measures related to deconcentration and decentralization total $372 million.

The action plan appears to supersede the PDNA, but that is not entirely clear, as the PDNA is characterized as an annex to the action plan. Regardless of their lack of harmonization, both would benefit from drawing more clearly on the fairly comprehensive framework program rather than just referring to it in passing. Like the framework program, both fail to address public-finance management and procurement, even though these have been important yet incomplete areas of public-administration reform.

Private Sector Economic Forum Draft Vision and Road Map. While not an official plan, the Private Sector Economic Forum's draft *Vision and Roadmap for Haiti*[32] includes some constructive ideas for increasing administrative capacity. In particular, it calls for support for Parliament, including funding for technical support for issue research, public hearings, and independent think tanks and institutions to provide reports and briefs to Parliament. It also suggests narrowing proposed constitutional reforms to two issues on which consensus is more achievable than broad reforms: permitting dual citizenship and stretching the electoral cycle from two to five years.

---

[32] This appraisal is based on the draft version of March 16, 2010.

Recommendations

Determine the Applicable Postearthquake Reform Plan

The framework program, the action plan, and the PDNA provide three different versions of a basis for crafting an updated public-administration reform and restructuring plan. A decision should be made quickly concerning which plan will be considered authoritative and thus should be used as the basis for further elaboration (the action plan or PDNA) or prioritization and updating (the framework program). *As the framework program is the most comprehensive and thoughtfully prepared of the three, it would serve best as a basis for further planning.*

Prioritize and Rationalize the Framework Program

Given the vast scope of the framework program (249 subcomponents), the Haitian government, in conjunction with donors, should set priorities, determine who is responsible for which actions, sequence measures for implementation, and organize a reduced number of tasks into a more realistic time frame. As a matter of urgency, donors should fund technical assistance for government planning (probably led by the prime minister's office, given its role in central public administration) to update and prioritize the subcomponents of the framework program. In addition, reform activities under way in public-finance management, procurement, and anticorruption should be folded into the scope of the framework program, even though those activities are under the purview of the Ministry of Economy and Finance rather than the prime minister's office. Perhaps because overly ambitious plans lose their currency when not being actively implemented, there may be a tendency to overlook useful plans that can be given new life.[33] Clearly, a great deal of effort was spent on developing the framework program; it need not be set aside even with the changed circumstances.

---

[33] In 2009, the UN Secretary-General's report on the Haiti mission urged the government to adopt a "blueprint for State reform"—without mentioning the government's Framework Program for State Reform, drafted with UNDP help (UN Security Council, 2009b, pp. 14–15).

Focus Attention and Resources on Civil Service Reform

Civil service reform is likely to face strong political challenge because of the prospect of reducing patronage opportunities and will take considerable time to implement. Nevertheless, efforts in this area should commence, beginning by clarifying who is in the civil service and what they are doing and by creating a system for tracking civil servants. Ultimately, *building a competent and rationalized civil service is critical to building a more effective state.* Attracting new talent, improving the quality of existing civil servants (through training and enforcement of performance standards), and building human-resource management tools and systems (including job classifications, standards and procedures for hiring and firing, a merit promotion system, salary grades, and clarified career ladders) should be among the highest priorities for public-administration reform. Emphasis also should be placed on creating a financial incentive system for good performance. With no job descriptions, and no standards and procedures yet in place for performance evaluation, promotion, or dismissal from office, government employees have few incentives to perform competently. Also, *consideration should be given to creating a fast-track program with enhanced salaries and prestige for highly qualified young people willing to enter and commit to at least several years of public service.*

Initiate Practical Steps Toward Decentralization and Deconcentration

Decentralization and deconcentration are perennially on the political agenda, yet very little progress has been made in realizing these objectives. Despite the enhanced attention to these topics in the action plan, it is not evident that political commitment to decentralization and deconcentration is any greater now than before the earthquake. Efforts toward addressing the technical aspects may not make great strides until a genuine political consensus on decentralization and deconcentration is built; nevertheless, practical work can be done to prepare the ground. *If the Préval administration is indeed committed to these objectives, it should work expeditiously both to build a political consensus and, using executive decrees if necessary, to push forward the practical aspects of the processes.*

The most important practical step needed is to more clearly define the respective roles and authorities of the several levels of government. Ultimately, this will require legislation. To begin the process, however, progress could be made without legislation in clarifying the roles of officials performing deconcentrated functions and in giving those officials the resources and logistical means to carry out their responsibilities. Donors could be influential in promoting decentralization and deconcentration by consulting and working directly with local officials and by distributing their resources in a way that bolsters local government.

Offer Support to Parliament and Political Parties

Haiti's parliament does not work well. As an independent branch of government, solutions cannot be imposed on Parliament. But *the executive branch and donors should offer technical and material assistance to improve Parliament's working conditions, staffing, and ability to prepare legislation.* The recommendations of the Private Sector Economic Forum are a useful contribution in this regard. In addition, *donors should offer technical assistance to political parties to improve their organizational structures and abilities to engage with constituents.* Donors should include political parties in reconstruction planning processes as a means of building their capabilities.

Keep Constitutional Reform Modest for Now

Constitutional reform is a significant undertaking in any circumstances. Given the Haitian public's suspicion of government and the contentious nature of some of the issues that have been discussed as possible topics of reform (such as re-creating the army and extending the presidential term limit), Haiti would benefit from conducting constitutional reform in an open, transparent, and broadly inclusive way. A process of this nature could not be conducted quickly and would consume considerable political capital. *In the current context of a wide array of political imperatives, initiatives to reform the constitution should be kept modest.* The Private Sector Economic Forum's recommendation—focus on permitting dual citizenship and lengthening the electoral cycle—accords with the apparent consensus on the most urgent issues.

Employ Donor Leverage to Secure Key Reforms

State-building in Haiti will require a discreet but very hands-on approach to political reform by the major donors. This does not mean explicitly conditioning assistance on performance, a technique that has seldom produced meaningful political improvement. Indeed, Haitian politicians have repeatedly shown themselves ready to reject even gigantic aid packages if these came at the cost of some perceived domestic political advantage. Rather than conditions-based assistance, aid will need to be used to more subtly grease the political wheels of reform, bolstering the position and influence of its champions and rewarding those who effectively advance the agenda.

This means that *projects need to be evaluated not just on their ability to increase GDP or decrease poverty but also on their capacity to reconcile competing interests, secure political goals of importance to the donor community, and thereby redirect the competition for wealth and power found in any society into channels more likely to benefit this particular society.* Leverage of this sort is likely to produce results only if the donors are united and if they prove capable of exercising their potentially massive influence in quiet, discreet, and subtle ways in support of the relatively few really essential reforms, particularly those requiring parliamentary action, covered herein.

CHAPTER FOUR

Justice

The Challenges

Haiti's justice system is extremely flawed: The courts do not carry out their constitutional responsibilities; laws are not applied and procedures are not followed; the criminal code dates from the early 19th century; prison conditions are horrific; legal aid barely exists; legal professionals are inadequately educated; corruption is widespread; and relations are poor between the HNP on the one hand and prosecutors and judges on the other. In short, Haiti has no cognizable "system" of justice. Various plans and initiatives to address these problems since the mid-1990s have borne little fruit.

Justice-system formation and reform are typically slow and especially complex aspects of state-building,[1] and Haiti has been no exception. The multiplicity of actors—the Ministry of Justice and Public Security (Ministère de la Justice et de la Sécurité Publique, or MJSP), nominally independent judges, prosecutors, the prison administration, the private bar, and law schools—and the need for linkages between the police and justice actors make coherence and coordination in reform-strategy planning and implementation difficult to achieve. The struggle over judicial independence between the executive branch and the judiciary undermines collaboration. For judges, a fine balance has to be struck between instituting accountability and ensuring independence. Moreover, unlike the police, the justice system does not have a unified command structure through which reforms can be carried out.

[1] See Jensen (2008, pp. 119–120, 124–125).

And unlike such areas as health and education, there are no gap-filling private or nongovernmental alternatives to a state-run justice system.[2] In addition, a functioning justice system requires skilled and educated legal professionals, and these are in short supply in Haiti.

Long-Standing Challenges

One way to view the challenges of reforming the justice system in Haiti is to identify the system's institutional, procedural, infrastructure, human-resource, and fiscal-resource weaknesses. Viewed this way, the justice system is riddled with challenges. Many judges have no legal education, and some are illiterate. There is no criminal-record system, so it is impossible to know whether a suspect has a prior record or is wanted in another jurisdiction. The courts operate in French, but only about 20 percent of the population speaks French. Haiti has no functioning forensic laboratory. The laws do not permit plea-bargaining or alternative sentencing for minor crimes. Judicial-appointment procedures are not followed. Many courthouses are in poor condition.[3]

Perhaps the most glaring manifestation of the justice system's dysfunction is the situation in Haiti's prisons. An estimated 75–85 percent of the prison population is being held in illegally prolonged pretrial detention; many of these prisoners have never seen a judge. At least some have been detained longer than they ever could have been sentenced.[4] For cases that are brought to trial, the conviction rate is a stunningly low 3 percent. As one longtime observer noted, some people are arrested in Haiti for literally nothing,[5] though the low conviction rate also suggests poor case preparation.

---

[2] Individuals and communities fill gaps in access to justice at the local level through informal means of dispute resolution.

[3] Numerous reports describe the weaknesses of the justice system. See, e.g., International Crisis Group (2008, pp. 17–19; 2007a); Fleury (2007, p. 83); ILAC (2005); and World Bank (2006).

[4] The United Nations reported that more than 76 percent of detainees nationwide and more than 86 percent in the national penitentiary were being held in pretrial detention as of September 2009 (UN Security Council, 2009b, p. 10). In discussions with the RAND research team, experts cited slightly different figures.

[5] Discussion with NGO representative, Port-au-Prince, April 21, 2010.

Conditions in Haiti's prisons are horrendous as well: They are severely overcrowded and understaffed. Health care and sanitation are lacking. Security is insufficient, resulting in periodic riots and escapes.[6] The extreme disproportion of prisoners in pretrial detention and, thus, to some extent, the problem of overcrowding are consequences of the slow and inefficient court system. However, reforming the judiciary alone would not solve the prison problem. Greater enforcement of Haiti's laws and a more effective justice system—with better investigations and more successful prosecutions—could well increase the number of convicts. Although the prisons are bulging (occupancy is 335 percent of official capacity), Haiti's incarceration rate is the lowest in the Caribbean and the lowest but for three countries in all of the Americas.[7] More and modernized prison space is urgently needed.[8]

Haiti's judiciary lacks both mechanisms to ensure accountability and genuine independence. The judiciary is subordinate to the MJSP, though judges resist actual oversight. While corruption, absences, and low skills are widespread problems among judges, even those who are committed to their work struggle to function in the prevailing conditions.[9] The courts lack management systems for moving cases through the required procedural stages; collection of evidence by the police is often inadequate; and judicial infrastructure is in a general state of disrepair.

Looking at the challenges in terms of the abundant weaknesses of the justice system, there is virtually no end to the projects that can be imagined to repair the system's deficiencies. Strategies aiming to fix many of these problems simultaneously seem appealing, but such approaches have generated few results. Efforts and resources become too broadly dispersed across a wide range of projects.

---

[6] Discussion with foreign donor representative, Port-au-Prince, April 23, 2010; International Crisis Group (2007b).

[7] King's College London (2010). See also MJSP (2007).

[8] Canada is funding construction of a 750-person–capacity prison, expected to be completed by summer 2010.

[9] Discussion with NGO representative, Port-au-Prince, April 21, 2010.

Another way to approach these challenges is to focus on the problems the various weaknesses have produced—in other words, the effects of the system's failures and the issues that the justice system should address but does not. The problems are no less grave when approached from this perspective, but their diagnosis can be more precise and the priorities for action more easily identified.

Taking this approach, the most glaring long-standing challenge is prolonged pretrial detention. Prolonged detention is, in large part, due to slow-moving court procedures and inadequate recordkeeping, although police bear part of the blame. Another key challenge is lack of access to justice. Costs, the locations of courts, the language barrier due to the use of French, and long judicial delays are among the factors that constrain access. A third major problem is the lack of basic data about people who have been arrested, cases, and court dockets. The lack of a system of information management, poor training, and weak communication procedures among different actors in the system have resulted in chaos. Many judges do not even know the number of cases on their own dockets, and there is no respect for legally required procedural timelines.

Justice reform in Haiti, as elsewhere, has a political dimension: Since coming to office, President Préval has yet to appoint a president of the supreme court (cour de cassation).[10] Préval's failure to make this appointment has stymied the creation of the Superior Council of the Judiciary (Conseil Supérieur du Pouvoir Judiciaire). Formally created by law in November 2007, this body is supposed to play a central role in setting rules for and exercising oversight over the judiciary. It is a key means for improving the courts and enhancing judicial independence. Because the president of the supreme court serves as chairperson of the council, the council cannot yet operate. Due to political tensions between the executive and the judiciary, the MJSP's judicial inspection service also does not function well.[11]

---

[10] UN Security Council (2009b, pp. 8–9).

[11] Discussions with Haitian government official and Haitian lawyer, Port-au-Prince, April 22, 2010.

Considerable international support has been provided for justice reform in Haiti in the past, to little effect. The lack of results has been due both to the Haitian government's unwillingness to carry out reforms and to poor program implementation on the part of donors. A U.S. government assessment of the impact of its nearly $27 million in assistance to the Haitian judicial sector from 1993 to 2000 found little to show for the investment, principally because of the Haitian government's lack of commitment to and follow-through in implementing reform.[12] A UNDP evaluation found that international investments of expertise and money in establishing justice in Haiti after 1994 failed in large part because donors were overly optimistic and naïve about the prospects of importing a modern justice system and ignored limitations in the capacity of Haitian institutions to absorb technical assistance and adopt changes.[13]

Consequences of the Earthquake

The earthquake did not fundamentally alter the long-standing challenges of justice reform, but it did add to the burden, principally in terms of loss of personnel, damage to infrastructure, and loss of files and equipment. The MJSP, supreme court, several other courthouses, and offices of some other justice-related bodies were destroyed. This damage reduced the already-limited institutional capacity of the justice system.[14]

The earthquake created some new challenges in terms of the type and volume of disputes requiring resolution. The government's PDNA notes that the earthquake "is going to lead to many civil law disputes, which will be made more difficult by the absence of land registry records and problems with birth, marriage and death registrations."[15] Only about 5 percent of land is registered in Haiti, and land registers

---

[12] GAO (2000). By comparison, the United States spent $65 million on assistance to the Haitian police from 1995 to 1999.

[13] UNDP (2003).

[14] See Republic of Haiti (2010a, p. 45).

[15] Republic of Haiti (2010b, p. 39).

were not reliable before the earthquake.[16] Moreover, many people did not have birth, death, or other identifying records before the earthquake; fewer do now.[17] Most of those killed in the earthquake were buried without certification of death, and many survivors lost whatever documents they had. The situation in Haiti is likely to be comparable to that in areas affected by the December 2004 Indian Ocean tsunami, in which thousands of property-distribution, inheritance, and guardianship cases emerged. Without proof of identity, people could not access money in bank accounts and insurance policies. Physical reconstruction was hampered by uncertainties and disputes about property rights and boundaries.[18]

Appraisal of Plans and Initiatives for Addressing the Challenges

Plans and Initiatives Before the Earthquake

There has been no shortage of reform plans, commissions, and working groups concerning Haiti's justice system, although implementation has been wanting.[19] The principal plans and initiatives of the post-Aristide period are appraised in this section.

MJSP Five-Year Plan. The MJSP's current five-year plan identifies many of the problems in the justice system and lays out principles, aspirations, and goals for improving the system.[20] It identifies some specific needs, such as training, improvement in the living standards and career guarantees for judicial personnel, and development of mecha-

---

16 Discussion with representative of international organization, Washington, D.C., March 18, 2010.

17 The OAS has been working on development of a civil registry in Haiti since 2005 and helped to create the Office of National Identification within the MJPS. Under this program, 4.3 million adults had been registered and issued identity cards prior to the earthquake, registration of children began a year ago, and death registration had been planned.

18 Stephens (2009, pp. 132–133).

19 See Fleury (2007, pp. 11–14).

20 MJSP (2006).

nisms for release pending trial to avoid prolonged pretrial detention. The plan sets out a list of priorities, such as adopting a code of ethics for judges, modernizing several legal codes, strengthening judicial security, transcribing customary law, and creating specialized courts. The document provides a broad vision for the development of the justice system but does not set timelines, sequencing, or benchmarks to guide implementation.

Some objectives emphasized by the government and donors have been achieved since 2006—in particular, the adoption in 2007 of three laws aimed at enhancing judicial independence and accountability.[21] These laws have not yet been implemented, however.[22]

GPRSP (2008–2010). Among governance issues, the GPRSP "accords priority" to justice and security.[23] It treats this area summarily, however. The justice portion of the GPRSP consists of a page-long list of institutional and logistical problems and another brief list of principles, goals, and priority areas of activity, such as "restructuring of the MJSP" and "strengthening of the judiciary branch." The paper does not propose a strategy or specific priorities for justice-system reform.

Recommendations of the Advisory Commission on Prolonged Pretrial Detention. This commission, established in June 2007 to examine and contribute to resolving the problem of prolonged pretrial detention, produced a final report in March 2008 that lays out a set of recommendations concerning the roles of the MJSP, police, Directorate of Penitentiary Administration (Direction Administrative Pénitentiaire, or DAP), judges, and prosecutors.[24] The recommendations are better described as detailed descriptions of the failures that have led to prolonged detention than as solutions to the problem. For example, the recommendations identify laws, rules, and deadlines that are not being respected and call for them to be followed. They pinpoint dysfunctional aspects of the justice system and urge that they be remedied.

---

[21] These laws concern establishment of the Superior Council of the Judiciary, the status of magistrates, and the magistrates' school.

[22] Discussion with Haitian government official, Port-au-Prince, April 22, 2010.

[23] Republic of Haiti (2007, pp. 49–51).

[24] CCDPP (2008, pp. 33–40).

While the recommendations may be helpful in diagnosing the problem of prolonged detention and they suggest that the problem would be solved if justice-system actors performed their roles as they should and had proper training, they do not propose practical steps toward solving the problem.

DAP Strategic Development Plan. This plan, developed with advice from foreign experts, is comprehensive and detailed. It discusses the problems in the prison system—in particular, the need for increased capacity—and provides a vision for the system in 2012.[25] The plan sets a broad goal (modernization of the prison system), several more concrete objectives, and a six-point program with numerous subsidiary tasks for pursuing those objectives. Four annexes addressing infrastructure improvements, equipment procurement, personnel management and training, and treatment of detainees specify projects and their expected results, general time frames, and costs. Among the more-expensive projects are prison construction and rehabilitation, recruitment and training of 800 new corrections officers, and improvement of prison admission procedures.

The plan is ambitious, though it claims not to be overly so. The gap between the projects and tasks envisioned and the actual pace of reform is large. As of September 2009, "limited progress was made in the implementation" of the plan, and prison conditions continued to deteriorate as overcrowding increased.[26] The plan included training of 270 new corrections officers in 2009, for example, but the government did not select the recruits.[27] Some work is under way on prison infrastructure building and improvement, though the extent is limited in relation to the overall need.

Working Group on Reform of the Criminal and Criminal Procedure Codes. Haiti's criminal and criminal-procedure codes date from 1835 and were among the Napoleonic Codes transplanted from France. Though they have been supplemented by a variety of laws and decrees over the years, they still reflect the conditions of 19th-century

25 MJSP (2007).

26 UN Security Council (2009b, pp. 9–10).

27 UN Security Council (2009b, p. 10).

France and are, to say the least, outdated. As part of a broader emphasis on law reform, President René Préval established a working group on reform of the criminal and criminal-procedure codes, under the leadership of former justice minister René Magloire; the working group has developed draft codes.[28] Because of the postponement of parliamentary elections due to the earthquake, adoption of these codes will not be considered before 2011.

This is one of several specialized working groups or commissions that Préval has established, and one that appears to be producing results. While the work being undertaken is useful, given the serious deficiencies of the existing codes, the revised codes, if adopted, will have an effect only if judges and lawyers are trained to understand them and begin applying them.

Revised Plans

The government's March 2010 *Action Plan for National Recovery and Development*[29] and the annexed PDNA briefly and in general terms lay out an approach to reconstructing the justice system that is "based on getting services for the prevention of violence and attention to the needs of the population back into working order, and beginning a thorough reform."[30] The PDNA observes that the justice system before the earthquake "was not very effective" and that prior reforms had little effect.

The documents call for reestablishing and reinforcing existing operations, guaranteeing access to justice for affected communities, and "starting a process of structural reform of the Haitian justice system." A draft work plan for the MJSP for March 2010 through September 2011 spells out some of the activities, costs, and other details related to those three objectives. The PDNA also calls for developing a plan to modernize the prison system, without acknowledging the existence of such a plan. These documents should be regarded only as preliminary

---

[28] Albrecht, Aucoin, and O'Connor (2009, pp. 2, 5).

[29] Republic of Haiti (2010a).

[30] Republic of Haiti (2010b, p. 40).

statements of the government's intentions, given their limited provisions concerning the justice system.

Recommendations

The failures of the justice system and the steps that should be taken to address them are well understood among senior advisers to the Haitian government and within the donor community. Nevertheless, the government has found itself unable—or unwilling—to take those steps in light of elite opposition. Political boldness and consistent donor pressure will be needed to make headway on reforms that have so far largely languished.

To eventually create a functional justice system, thorough reform—or, where capabilities do not exist, formation—will be needed in every element of the system, including legal education, the courts, MJSP administration, legal aid, law codes, and corrections. Access to justice will have to be improved; procedural and substantive laws will have to be applied as envisioned; and sustainable and reliable levels of financing will have to be made available to attract well-qualified legal professionals to public service and to maintain adequate infrastructure. Perhaps most challenging, building a system of justice that works in the public's interest will require more adherence to the rule of law within government institutions and the broader environment. These should remain the long-term goals, but, given current conditions in Haiti and the challenges discussed in this chapter, none will be fully realized within the next three to five years, even assuming political commitment to reform.

Resources and political capital in the near to medium term should be expended on a few critical areas in which practical progress could be made and that directly concern urgent needs of the Haitian population. Although a handful of successful reform initiatives will not transform the entire justice system, moving from a situation in which *almost nothing* works to one in which *some* things actually work would be a major achievement. Concentrating on a few initiatives would not require abandoning all other reform projects; those that are well advanced, such as the government's criminal law and criminal-procedure code reform process, should be completed. If and when the political logjam is broken, the Superior Council of the Judiciary should be brought into operation and supported. However, we recommend that the government of Haiti and the international community adopt the priorities outlined in the rest of this section.

Devote Greater Attention to Justice Reform

First and foremost, the Haitian government and donors should place much higher priority on planning and carrying out justice reform, giving it priority even over strengthening the police force. Past governments failed to capitalize on donors' investments in justice programs; even now, there are some worrying signs that the current government may not be sufficiently committed to reform, such as the very long delay in appointing a supreme-court president. Donors have tended to give other sectors higher priority, including, particularly, the police, despite the fact that those latter reforms will ultimately founder in the absence of progress in the justice sector. It must be acknowledged, however, that justice reform progress is not merely a function of the amount of funding provided—past experience indicates that more projects will not automatically produce more progress. Clarification of priorities, realistic strategic planning, and a strong political commitment are essential first steps toward more-effective reform.

Create a Mechanism for Resolving Real and Other Property Disputes Stemming from the Earthquake

Property disputes (including disputes over land, bank accounts, and other assets) are likely to mushroom in the aftermath of the earthquake. The Haitian public will need means of resolving such disputes quickly. *Given how slowly the court system operates and the constraints on access to it, a property-dispute resolution mechanism should be established outside of the court system, under the authority of the MJSP.* It would need to be staffed by specially trained personnel, but not all would need to be lawyers. The mechanism could be based on an alternative dispute resolution model, and disputants could be represented at no or low cost by paralegals trained for this purpose. Operations should be decentralized. In addition to bringing dispute resolution closer to those who need it, decentralization could ensure sound decisionmaking; people in communities know each other, the lay of the land, and the facts related to such disputes.

To manage this initiative, the MJSP would require sustained technical assistance in structuring the mechanism (drawing on examples from other postconflict and postdisaster situations), drafting procedures, hiring and preparing personnel, and publicizing the new mechanism. Particular attention will need to be paid to devising accountability and oversight mechanisms to mitigate opportunities for corruption. Implementation of the initiative could have long-term institution-building benefits, such as strengthening the MJSP's management capabilities. The training and use of paralegals as advocates provided to all parties could provide a model on which to build later, as Haiti is short of legal advocates for people who cannot afford lawyers. This initiative should not be approached as a pilot project, with limited potential impact and limited-duration commitment to funding, but as a full-scale effort.

Establish a Special Ad Hoc Panel for Detainee Review

Haiti's prisons need to be cleared of people who should not be there; the courts have proven incapable of addressing this long-standing problem. Ultimately, the most durable way to ensure that people in Haiti's prisons are being held legally is for the courts to function as they are supposed to and for judges to apply the law. But addressing prolonged pretrial detention cannot wait for significant progress in judicial reform.

A special, ad hoc panel for detainee review should be established as an administrative body under the MJSP with the power to review cases and, if appropriate, order releases. Arguably, Parliament should authorize this by law, but, as people are being held in pretrial detention because current laws are not being obeyed, there is an attractive argument for authorizing such a panel by decree, in the interest of fairness.

So that prisons do not continue to fill up with pretrial detainees, establishing the panel should be combined with requiring that all arrest warrants be given an expiration date in accordance with procedural time-

lines.[31] More-rigorous review and authorization procedures within the HNP before arrests are made are likely to be needed as well. Early completion of the prisoner database currently being populated would be a complementary measure; such a database is needed, among other things, to keep track of release dates.

Two somewhat similar but limited-scale detainee review initiatives have been tried in the past in Haiti, but implementation was criticized in one instance[32] and not sustained in the other.[33]

Expand Prison Capacity

The capacity and conditions of Haiti's prisons are woefully inadequate and undermine any prospect of building a reasonably effective and rights-respecting justice system. *Prison infrastructure rehabilitation and new construction should be given much higher priority than such efforts have received to date.* The DAP's strategic development plan for 2007–2012, drafted with assistance from Canada, provides a starting point for developing the details of a program to expand prison capacity, but it is very ambitious and should be reformulated into a more realistic plan. Prison construction is an expensive undertaking and will require external funding.

Build an Information-Management System

A unified information-management system that police, prosecutors, courts, and prisons can use should be established. The limited database being put in place for the prison system (with UNDP support) may provide a basis on which to build a system that includes a single case file for each individual, from arrest through incarceration. Accompanying this

---

[31] This idea is drawn from the recommendations of the Consultative Commission on Prolonged Pretrial Detention discussed earlier.

[32] The Consultative Commission on Prolonged Pretrial Detention, which operated from June 2007 to April 2008, reviewed cases in the Ouest department and in Gonaïves and obtained the release of some detainees, but police and human-rights organizations criticized its work (International Crisis Group, 2008, p. 19).

[33] In the late 1990s, a courtroom was set up in the national penitentiary in order to facilitate review of cases of prolonged pretrial detention, but the Haitian government did not sustain the NGO-initiated program.

initiative, investigating judges should be required to provide written justifications—noted in the case file—for holding suspects longer than 48 hours.

This technical initiative would be foundational for other, more-fundamental changes in the justice system. For example, judges cannot be held to account for delays and backlogs without access to information about cases on their docket (how many, how long pending, and the procedural deadlines that apply). An effective case-management system, which would identify relevant deadlines, could be used to foster expectations that procedures will be followed within the legally required timelines. In addition, a unified system could build communication links among police, prosecutors, and courts. The MJSP and the Superior Council of the Judiciary (if and when it becomes operational) could use data extracted from such a system as a management tool. And data about what is actually happening in the justice system (and not happening), if made transparent as they should be, could help create social demand for reforms.

CHAPTER FIVE

Security

The Challenges

Long-Standing Challenges

Efforts to reform the security sector in Haiti have faced three main, related challenges. First, the security situation is volatile, and the state has very limited ability to assert its authority vis-à-vis criminal networks, drug traffickers, armed gangs, and other spoilers.[1] In 1994, after a U.S.-led intervention to reinstall the elected president, Jean-Bertrand Aristide, the Haitian military was abolished. Since then, the HNP has been the only state institution in the country to provide internal or external security. It has been responsible for performing a broad array of functions beyond basic community policing: counternarcotics, border protection, maritime patrolling, quasi-military tasks, and guarding the prisons. In these areas, the HNP has heavily depended on the military and police forces of MINUSTAH, deployed in 2004.

Second, the government has not demonstrated a consistent commitment to police reform. Cooperation between MINUSTAH and the interim government of Prime Minister Gérard Latortue proved difficult in 2004 and 2005, as the prime minister did not support police reforms. The government was itself accused of being involved in violating the law and human rights.[2] After the election of President René

---

[1] See UN Security Council (2009b, p. 5); International Crisis Group (2008, p. 2).

[2] See Lindsay (2006, p. 32) and Mobekk (2008, p. 116).

Préval in February 2006, the Haitian government was more supportive of police reform.

Third, the institutions of the HNP are poorly developed. Since its creation at the end of 1994, the HNP has been prone to political abuse and corruption and has lacked the manpower, equipment, training, and professional standards to provide security for the population.[3] In mid-2006, when police reform began in earnest, the HNP still consisted of only 7,000 police officers, virtually all of them badly equipped and poorly trained.[4] The HNP has also lacked basic institutional capabilities, such as keeping records on current and former police officers, financial management, and internal control. Low salaries and poor working conditions for the majority of police officers have contributed to corruption and criminal activity within the force.[5]

In his last report on Haiti before the earthquake, UN Secretary-General Ban Ki-moon stated that the Haitian police force "still lacks the force levels, training, equipment and managerial capacity" to respond effectively to Haiti's internal security threats without external assistance.[6] This has been especially true outside of Port-au-Prince. Departmental capitals and rural areas, where police often have to cover large swaths of territory with few roads and little staff, have long been neglected in the police reform efforts.[7]

An additional major problem is the weak link between the police and the judiciary. The lack of meaningful judicial reform and the very poor coordination and collaboration among the police, prosecutors, and courts have the potential to undermine progress on police reform.[8]

---

3 See Mendelson-Forman (2006, p. 22).

4 See "Haitian National Police Reform Plan" (2006, p. 3). This plan was adopted by the government of Haiti on August 8, 2006.

5 See "UN Special Envoy Says Haiti in Urgent Need of Police" (2006).

6 UN Security Council (2009b, p. 5).

7 See International Crisis Group (2008, p. 8).

8 See Call (2009, p. 14) and Fortin and Pierre (2008, p. 20).

Consequences of the Earthquake

The January 12 earthquake severely set back efforts to build the HNP. The immediate effect was felt in the loss of personnel and the destruction of buildings and other infrastructure needed for police operations.

The HNP lost some 80 police officers, and 250 officers were injured.[9] The earthquake also further weakened the modest police presence outside of Port-au-Prince because officers had to be redeployed from other provinces to the capital.[10] The earthquake destroyed an estimated 45 percent of the police stations in Port-au-Prince and its surroundings, including the HNP headquarters.[11]

While fewer officers were available as a consequence of the earthquake, the demands on the police force were greater than usual, given the need to protect Haitians and property against looters, ensure public order in the tent camps, and protect the most vulnerable.[12] In addition, some 5,000 detainees, or 60 percent of Haiti's prison population—among them many gang leaders and members who had been arrested since 2007—escaped in the chaos of the earthquake.[13]

Appraisal of Plans and Initiatives for Addressing the Challenges

Plans and Initiatives Before the Earthquake

The international community has been involved in building and reforming Haiti's security sector since the beginning of the 1990s. Both the United States in the 1990s and the United Nations then and since have seen police reform as essential to the departure of their own soldiers and police. In the aftermath of the U.S.-led Operation Restore Democracy to reinstall President Aristide, an Interim Public Security

---

[9] Discussion with HNP official, Port-au-Prince, April 23, 2010.

[10] See International Crisis Group (2010, p. 11).

[11] International Crisis Group (2010, p. i).

[12] See Republic of Haiti (2010b, p. 39).

[13] See International Crisis Group (2010, p. 10).

Force for Haiti was created, which eventually evolved into the HNP. The United States, the UN, and the Haitian government began a campaign to recruit and train new police forces, and a police school was established. Despite early progress, the overall process of police reform was not successful: No police force can remain honest and efficient when embedded in a corrupt and incompetent judicial and political system.

Police reform resumed in earnest only in 2006 after the election of President Préval. Since then, national and international efforts have centered on the HNP reform plan that the Haitian government adopted in August 2006. The international community's contribution to restoring and maintaining a stable security environment in Haiti and to reforming Haiti's security sector has pursued a double-track approach. On one track, MINUSTAH's military and civilian police components conduct operations with the HNP against individuals and groups that threaten internal security where the HNP is unable to do so alone. MINUSTAH seeks to strengthen the HNP's capacity through joint patrolling and operations.

In the second track, the UN, other international organizations, and bilateral donors have attempted to build the HNP and the administrative structures that govern it through monitoring, mentoring, advising, training, equipping, and institutional capacity-building. The concept underlying this double-track approach is that the UN peacekeepers and police will scale down their role as the Haitian police become increasingly capable of exercising their law-enforcement responsibilities. To pursue both tracks, the UN Security Council initially authorized the deployment of 6,700 military troops and 1,622 civilian police and has, several times, increased those numbers; as of June 2010, 8,940 military and 4,391 police personnel were authorized.[14]

The United States and Canada are the most important bilateral donors in the area of police and justice in Haiti. The U.S. State Department funds 50 U.S. police and corrections advisers and provides significant support for HNP training.[15] The Canadian government supports

14 MINUSTAH (undated).

15 See U.S. Department of State (undated).

police reform through the Stabilization and Reconstruction Task Force (START), through which it deploys police officers to MINUSTAH and has, for instance, provided the inspectorate general of the HNP with offices.[16]

The ultimate aim of the 2006 reform plan was to create a police force of 14,000 well-trained, well-equipped officers by 2011 that would provide basic security for Haiti in line with international standards. The major reform objectives were to enhance recruitment, training, and vetting of police officers and to create administrative capacity. The plan identified specific numeric targets and timelines. The vetting process was to involve a full review of all HNP members by mid-2007. For 2007 and 2008, the plan also foresaw a review of the police force's employment conditions and salaries. In order to improve administrative capacity, the plan focused on the Office of the General Inspectorate, which is responsible for vetting and controlling the police force; on the Central Division of Administration and General Services;[17] and on the Central Directorates of the Judicial Police and the Police Administration.

The police reform plan had merit. It was jointly elaborated by the Haitian government and MINUSTAH and thus ensured a high degree of local ownership. It not only provided a strategic vision of the future police force but also contained agreed priorities, specific targets, and related timelines. Finally, the plan identified the estimated costs for wages related to the staffing targets, as well as for overall implementation of the reform (US$700 million). The plan was somewhat less explicit, however, on where these funds should come from: It was presumed that wages could be financed from the Haitian state budget, whereas the capital investment requirements (infrastructure, transport, communications, weapons, and training) would come from donor contributions or budget support.

The plan's objectives and priorities—to build a professional force for "essential" policing duties and the state institutions needed to con-

---

[16] See Foreign Affairs and International Trade Canada (2010).

[17] The Central Division of Administration and General Services is responsible for human resources, finances, and logistics of the HNP.

trol and manage it—were sound. The plan's authors acknowledged that a stronger police force—consisting of 18,000–20,000 police and other security officers—would be required to provide the full spectrum of security services, including a coast guard, border control, fire brigades, and personnel for the penal system.[18] By endorsing a more modest approach and a relatively limited mission for the country's only security service, the plan took into account the financial and other resource constraints that Haiti faced.[19] It is surely preferable in the short and medium terms to build a smaller but more professional and well-managed police force than to stretch resources thin.

While, on paper, the police reform plan was sound, the crucial question is the extent to which it has actually been implemented since 2006. From the perspective of numbers alone, there was considerable progress before the earthquake. In 2006, when the plan was made public, the HNP consisted of about 7,000 officers, up from only 2,500 in 2004. By March 2008, the number of serving officers had risen to 8,444,[20] to 9,247 by February 2009,[21] and to 9,715 by August of that same year.[22] Despite this progress, recruitment remained below what was needed to reach the goal of having 14,000 officers by 2011.[23]

Meeting the desired staffing levels for police officers depends on the availability of sufficient training facilities. Before the earthquake, the Haitian government and donors planned to expand the training capacities of the National Police School (Ecole Nationale de Police).[24] A

---

[18] See "Haitian National Police Reform Plan" (2006, p. 4). See also UN Security Council (2008, p. 6).

[19] This does not mean that the plan excludes the development of these more-encompassing capacities. Yet, the focus is clearly on the more modest goal of having a 14,000-strong police force for "essential policing functions." This number is also the basis of the cost calculations included in the plan.

[20] See UN Security Council (2008, p. 6).

[21] See UN Security Council (2009a, p. 7).

[22] See UN Security Council (2009b, p. 7).

[23] See International Crisis Group (2008, p. 1).

[24] See UN Security Council (2009a, p. 8; 2009b, p. 8).

new police academy for mid- and senior-ranking officers was planned as well but has not yet been set up.

Professionalization of the police force was the most important goal of the reform plan. The Haitian government and MINUSTAH agree that the HNP has made great strides in its professionalization and effectiveness. The Organisation for Economic Co-Operation and Development (OECD) cites opinion polls that indicated that 70 percent of the Haitian population considered the national police to be the most reliable state institution.[25] Foreign diplomats and other international observers were surprised by the fact that the HNP was able to show a strong presence in Port-au-Prince right after the devastating earthquake in January 2010. Despite these indications of enhanced professionalism, the HNP was still haunted by reports of excessive use of force, unlawful arrests, and poor-quality investigations.[26] Promotions based on contacts rather than merit had a demoralizing effect on officers who were passed over.[27]

Vetting of HNP officers and upper-level staff is a crucial tool to enhance the professionalism of the force. Ideally, vetting includes a review of an officer's education, criminal record, interaction with citizens, personal conduct, and personal income and assets.[28] By the beginning of 2008, close to 3,600 files had been opened—covering around 40 percent of the total number of HNP staff at the time—but only 223 files, or less than 3 percent of the total, were completed.[29] By September 2009, the last reporting date before the earthquake, 67 percent of all HNP officers were under review and more than 20 percent of the reviews had been completed.[30]

Despite these positive developments, the progress that has been made so far in the vetting process should be viewed with caution.

---

25 See OECD (undated [a], p. 9).

26 See UN Security Council (2009a, p. 11); see also UN Security Council (2009b, p. 11).

27 See CANADEM (2009, p. 6).

28 See CANADEM (2009, p. 11).

29 See UN Security Council (2008, p. 7).

30 See UN Security Council (2009b, p. 8).

Records on personal data tend to be very poor in Haiti, making it difficult to track police officers' past and present behavior (or misbehavior). Moreover, the final decision to remove disqualified officers from their duties remained with the Haitian authorities. There are indications that the upper-management level of the HNP was often reluctant to fully collaborate with investigators.[31] The weak link between the police and the judiciary posed another major impediment for the vetting process. The inspectorate general did not have the competencies and mechanisms in place to track the files on police officers that were submitted for possible prosecution.[32] While there have been some improvements in communication between the police and judges, problems remain.[33] These problems probably contributed to the fact that less than 5 percent of the officers vetted were actually declared unsuitable for the police service.[34] Whether the vetting process has been effective enough to actually purge the HNP of corrupt elements remains an open question.[35]

Improvement in the administrative support structures—most notably, the inspectorate general and the Central Directorate for Police Administration—is a precondition for durable reform. There has been progress in this area as well. According to a MINUSTAH official, the administrative capacity of the HNP had been strengthened before the earthquake. The payroll system worked reasonably well, and the police budget was more transparent and competently administered than in the past.[36] Despite this progress, the HNP still lacks sufficient middle- and senior-management capacity, as well as a personnel system ade-

---

[31] See CANADEM (2009, p. 32).

[32] See Fortin and Pierre (2008, p. 18).

[33] Discussion with HNP official, Port-au-Prince, April 23, 2010.

[34] Discussion with HNP official, Port-au-Prince, April 23, 2010. The UN Secretary-General, in his March 2008 report on the implementation of MINUSTAH's mandate, stated that, up to that point, 61 police recruits had been dismissed based on background checks. See UN Security Council (2008, p. 7). The reports of March and September 2009 do not provide specific numbers on this (UN Security Council, 2009a, 2009b).

[35] See International Crisis Group (2008, p. 9).

[36] Telephone conversation with MINUSTAH official, May 27, 2010.

quate to ensure that officers are rewarded or penalized based on their performance.[37]

In sum, the efforts to build and reform the police force in Haiti prior to the earthquake achieved tangible results, in particular in terms of increasing the number of officers and improving professionalism. Haitian and international actors agreed on a reform plan that was "strategic" in the sense that it included clear priorities, benchmarks, and timelines for implementation. Due to limited resources and the reality of the situation in Haiti, the stated objectives and priorities were less ambitious than they would have been under better circumstances. However, the reforms that were adopted and implemented were sound and corresponded to the most-important needs for improving the police force in the country. Major problems were primarily related to implementation, not the concepts on which the reforms were based. Six years after the deployment of MINUSTAH, Haiti still remained heavily dependent on external military and police forces for the provision of basic security. This dependency is reflected in the fact that the number of international troops and police deployed as part of MINUSTAH had increased rather than decreased even before the earthquake. The goal of transferring security responsibility fully into Haitian hands was still a distant prospect.

Implementation of the reform plan showed three major shortcomings. First, insufficient financial and human resources had been committed to the process.[38] This is especially true for institutional capacity-building. Donor efforts were overly focused on the numerical strength of the HNP without due regard for the administrative support structure needed to make the reform process viable in the long run. Even to achieve the numeric recruitment targets, more UN police with specialized skills were needed—for instance, to run the vetting process. Second, the reform process focused on Port-au-Prince and neglected other regions.[39] Police stations in departmental capitals and rural areas

---

[37] See CANADEM (2009, p. 1); International Crisis Group (2008, p. 20).

[38] For corresponding assessments, see UN Security Council (2009b, p. 8); Republic of Haiti (2010b, p. 39); and CANADEM (2009, p. 32).

[39] See OECD (undated [a], p. 9).

were often severely understaffed due to lack of resources or the absence of staff.[40] Centralizing recruitment and training was part of the problem. For instance, more than 80 percent of the recruits at the police school came from Port-au-Prince.[41] Third, police reform was not linked to reform of the justice system; the latter lagged far behind. While considerable efforts had been invested in the police, reform of the justice sector more broadly in the post-Aristide era had only recently begun.[42]

Revised Plans

Immediate concerns after the earthquake were to ensure public security and protect the most-vulnerable groups. To fill the enlarged gap between available police and the need for additional security forces, the international community reinforced its military and police presence after the earthquake. The United States temporarily deployed 7,500 military personnel,[43] while the European Union (EU) dispatched some 300 gendarmes.[44] One week after the earthquake, the UN Security Council authorized the deployment of 2,000 additional troops and 1,500 additional civilian police.[45]

Looking beyond these short-term concerns, the Haitian government, in its action plan of March 2010[46] set out three major objectives related jointly to police and justice reform. These are spelled out in more detail in a draft working plan for the MJSP for March 2010 to September 2011. The first objective relates to the immediate need to procure basic equipment lost in the earthquake and create temporary offices and support infrastructure for the MJSP, the HNP, and the DAP and to resume police training. The second objective is to guarantee access to justice and security for communities affected by the

---

40 See International Crisis Group (2008, p. 8).

41 See International Crisis Group (2008, p. 8).

42 For more details on this, see Chapter Four.

43 See Dorell (2010).

44 See "Danish Minister Unhappy with EU's Slow Dispatch of Police to Haiti" (2010).

45 See UN Security Council (2010).

46 Republic of Haiti (2010a).

earthquake and for those communities hosting displaced people. The third objective is to create favorable conditions for further reform and improved administration in justice and security in the longer run.[47]

In the action plan, as well as in the PDNA annexed to it, the Haitian government estimates the costs for recovery and reconstruction for the rule of law, justice, and security sectors at $255 million for 18 months plus another $200 million for three years.[48] It is not entirely clear how these numbers relate to the cost estimate ($700 million) provided in 2006 for implementation of the police reform plan.[49]

These measures and proposals to rebuild and reform the security sector after the earthquake raise several questions. The first is how Haiti's dependence on international military and police and on bilateral donor support for HNP operations can be gradually eliminated over the next several years. MINUSTAH ought to work to reinforce the role of the Haitian government in providing security so that the mission's role will decline over time. This is crucial for enhancing both the capacity and legitimacy of the Haitian state in the eyes of the population. So far, no strategy has been put in place to ensure the handover of responsibility from MINUSTAH to the Haitian government. Given Haiti's economic situation and dependence on donors, the Haitian government is unlikely to be in a position to fully fund HNP operations for a long time. The government's—as well as the Haitian parliament's—commitment to fund the HNP even to the extent of its ability has been unconvincing.[50]

The second question is how to translate the general goals laid out in the action plan and the PDNA into specific priorities and timelines. The action plan does not spell out how the 2006 reform plan should be adapted to the postearthquake situation. The one exception, in which

[47] Republic of Haiti (2010a, p. 45).

[48] See Republic of Haiti (2010a, p. 46; 2010b, p. 41).

[49] After the earthquake, MINUSTAH and the HNP conducted a needs assessment for the police sector. The assessment estimated that $270 million was needed to resume policing functions after the quake and to further implement the police reform plan of 2006 (telephone conversation with MINUSTAH official, May 27, 2010).

[50] Discussion with donor representative, Port-au-Prince, April 23, 2010.

the action plan specifically alters the 2006 plan, concerns the numeric targets for the HNP. Instead of the goal of 14,000 police officers by 2011, the action plan sets a target of 12,000 officers by 2010 and 16,000 officers by 2015. The Haitian government has thus stretched the process of building the HNP by four more years while modestly increasing the target for the end state.[51]

The third question is how police reform can be brought into line with the overall reconstruction strategy of the Haitian government and the international community. One of the major elements of this overall strategy is to decentralize government administration and services. Putting more emphasis on providing security and justice in the cities and rural areas outside of Port-au-Prince has implications for staffing levels, equipment, offices, administration and for the funding needed for these reforms. These expenditures ought to be reflected in new plans.

The fourth question is how security and justice reforms can be better synchronized. In the past, progress made in reforming the police was countered by lack of progress in the judiciary and corrections. The police can work effectively only if they are complemented by functioning prosecutors, courts, and corrections. Future efforts to rebuild security and justice in Haiti need to better translate this insight into practice.

Recommendations

Since 2004, efforts to build a professional, effective Haitian police force have produced tangible results. In 2004, the force was widely seen as weak, corrupt, and politicized. In the face of domestic turmoil, the force melted down to 2,500 officers after the fall of the Aristide administration. Since then, the police force has evolved into a more effective

---

[51] See Republic of Haiti (2010a, p. 45). The HNP leadership was not consulted in developing the numbers (discussion with HNP official, Port-au-Prince, April 23, 2010). This is an indication of the lack of coordination and consultation within the Haitian government. It also raises the question of the extent to which the new numbers are based on a thorough assessment of the situation after the earthquake.

and credible organization: Force levels rose to more than 9,700 officers before the earthquake. Today, the HNP is much more trusted by the population than it used to be.

A major risk following the earthquake is that the Haitian government and the international donor community will fail to follow up on these past successes and lose focus on the police because of the many other needs stemming from the disaster. The provision of security remains a precondition for recovery and the improvement in the operations of the state. The most urgent need now is to replace personnel and reconstruct offices and other buildings that were destroyed during the quake. The national police school needs to be reopened as soon as possible. Beyond these immediate needs, the Haitian government and the international donor community ought to pursue the four priorities outlined here for building and reforming the HNP over the next five years.

Build on the 2006 Reform Plan and Adapt It to the Postearthquake Situation

The highest priority in the security sector should be to build on, adapt, and further implement the 2006 police reform plan. It offers a sound basis for building the HNP. Its focus is on basic and community policing, thus avoiding overburdening the force. Aside from increasing the numbers of officers, it identifies the most-important administrative structures and proposes ways to reinforce them. *The future strategy on police reform should focus on better implementation of this plan, including making sufficient financial resources available, while adapting it where necessary. As a first step, the benchmarks and timelines need to be adjusted.* So far, the postearthquake proposals—most notably the action plan of March 2010—have only spelled out adjustments to the numeric strength of the police force.

Second, police reform needs to be brought in line with the aim of decentralizing services and administration in Haiti. *If the aim is to provide services to the population as a whole and create regional development hubs, the police should be deployed accordingly.* Reversing centralization has implications for staffing levels, equipment, housing, and incentives for relocation of police officers. These implications have to be taken into account when adapting the police reform plan to the postearthquake situation.

Support Building Basic Administrative Structures

The police reform plan of 2006 emphasized the development of both operational and institutional capabilities. Implementation, however, has focused much more on enhancing the numeric strength of the police—in other words, on "getting uniforms on the street"—than on the institutional aspects of building a more resilient police organization. *Future strategies will have to create a better balance between these dimensions and investing more effort and resources in developing management systems and personnel to sustain the force.*

Specifically, the Office of the Inspector General, the Central Division of Administrative and General Services, and the Central Directorate of Police Administration require more support. *If the HNP does not develop basic administrative capabilities, none of the reforms undertaken will be sustainable.* Part of this agenda should be to improve the middle- and senior-management levels of the police force. To this end, the establishment of a police academy for middle- and senior-level officers, which has been planned for five years, should be a high priority.

Create Institutionalized Links Between Police and Justice

The link between the police and the judicial system has been a crucial weakness. Police and judicial reform have been disconnected; the latter has lagged far behind the former. Achieving a unified approach to policing and justice may seem unrealistic in the next five years, as it depends on substantial progress in the reform of Haiti's courts and penal system. *Pending a thorough judicial reform, the Haitian government and donors should support specific efforts on the police side of the equation that may mitigate the lack of a police-justice link.* For instance, a strengthened inspectorate general should have competencies and mechanisms to track files on police officers submitted to the judiciary for review. The inspectorate should press the judiciary for action on specific cases, rather than relying on the judiciary to track cases and initiate proceedings. The absence of such mechanisms has been a serious impediment to the vetting process. The HNP needs to establish communication channels with the judiciary rather than relying on personal relationships. The judicial police (the investigative arm of the HNP) needs to be strengthened and its training enhanced so that it is in a better position to prepare and take initiative in following up on criminal files presented to the courts.

Focus on a Police Force That the Haitians Need and Can Afford

Since its creation in 1994, Haiti's police force was given a broad range of responsibilities, including counternarcotics, border protection, maritime patrolling, some other quasi-military functions, and guarding the prisons. It took on these tasks by default: The HNP became Haiti's only security force after the military was abolished. In light of Haiti's economic conditions and poorly functioning government, the HNP could never realistically perform all these tasks. Against this background, the reform plan of 2006 rightly focused on improving basic policing capabilities. *Haiti and the international community should keep the focus on basic policing and on building Haitian ownership where police interact most directly with the population: on the streets and in the neighborhoods.* This would be an important contribution to enhance both the capacity and the legitimacy of the Haitian state.

Haiti will continue to be heavily dependent on the international community in security-related areas beyond basic policing, such as counternarcotics, border protection, maritime patrolling and responding to serious internal disturbances, as well as natural disasters. The Haitian government, the members of the United Nations Security Council, and the wider international donor community should acknowledge this reality and refrain from premature steps to reduce the international security presence.

To the extent possible, the Haitian government, with the support of international donors, should prepare the ground for assuming responsibility for the full spectrum of security functions. First and foremost, this would require a Haitian-led debate about the country's future security architecture. This could also include advanced planning and targeted security-assistance programs by bilateral donors in such areas as border patrol and crowd and riot control. *If state-building advances and if the economic situation improves, ambitions for the Haitian police or for creating additional security forces can be expanded accordingly.*

CHAPTER SIX

Economic Policy

The Challenges

Impoverishment

Haiti's primary economic challenge is generating economic growth. Haiti is the poorest country in the Western Hemisphere and the only country in the hemisphere formally designated a least-developed country by the World Bank. Alone among the states of the Western Hemisphere, per capita GDP in Haiti has fallen over the past 40 years to roughly one-half to two-thirds the level that it was in 1965. Not surprisingly, Haiti suffers from high rates of absolute poverty: Fifty-four percent of the population is estimated to live on less than $1 per day, and 72 percent on less than $2. Income distribution is the most unequal in the hemisphere.[1]

Poverty in Haiti is partially alleviated by the influx of remittances from Haitians who have emigrated, primarily to the United States and Canada. Some 30 percent of all households and 44 percent of metropolitan households receive remittances from friends or family members working abroad. Remittances account for about 30 percent of household income.[2] Private-sector transfers, primarily remittances, ran $1.25 billion in 2008, equivalent to 19 percent of GDP and 2.5 times exports.[3]

---

1 IHSI (2005, p. 19).

2 World Bank (2006, p. ii).

3 IMF (2010, p. 17).

Inflation

For Haiti to generate sustained economic growth, inflation will have to be contained. Haiti's track record on controlling inflation has been mixed. On the one hand, Haiti avoided the extraordinarily high inflation rates that a number of Latin American countries suffered during the 1970s. On the other hand, as can be seen in Figure 6.1, inflation rates have been high, running 20 percent between 1990 and 2000 and 15 percent in the subsequent decade. These rates are substantially higher than the hemispheric average for the past two decades and at a level that makes operating a business difficult.

Poor Business Environment

Haiti is poor in great part because of its difficult environment for business. In 2009, Haiti ranked 151 out of 183 countries in the world in terms of doing business (this ranking was published in 2010 prior to the earthquake).[4] The process of registering a business is one of the most

Figure 6.1
Inflation in Haiti

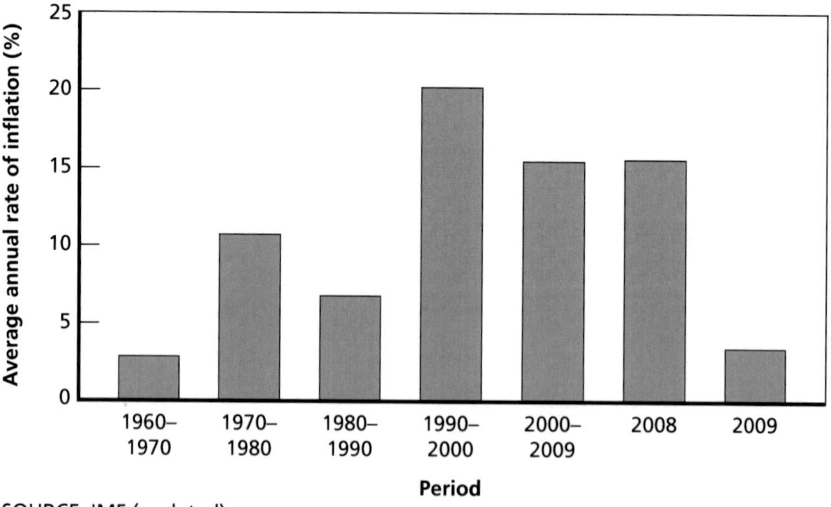

SOURCE: IMF (undated).
RAND *MG1039-6.1*

---

[4] World Bank (undated [b]).

difficult and lengthy in the world, taking an average of 195 days and entailing 13 separate procedures, and is relatively costly. Registering changes in title for property is even more onerous, running 405 days on average. Businesses also find a poor climate for investor protection; lengthy, burdensome procedures for obtaining construction permits; hurdles in engaging in foreign trade; difficulties in obtaining credit; and onerous procedures for closing a business.

The difficulties Haitians face in engaging in economic activity have stifled economic development. Sanctions imposed following the 1992 coup and political instability have also not helped. As a consequence of these problems, industry accounts for a relatively small 16 percent of GDP;[5] manufacturing runs 9 percentage points of this total. Manufacturing is concentrated in clothing, Haiti's most important export by far: Clothing accounts for 90 percent of Haiti's exports.[6] Despite Haiti's low-cost labor and proximity to and favorable customs treatment by the United States, exports run only 10 percent of GDP, although they have risen in most years since 2002.

Appraisal of Plans and Policies for Addressing the Challenges

Monetary Policy

Before the earthquake, the Haitian government had articulated a number of development goals and outlined a strategy for achieving those goals in its GPRSP, including goals for macroeconomic policies. Macroeconomic goals and policies are laid out in more detail in Haiti's three-year arrangement with the IMF under the Poverty Reduction and Growth Facility (PRGF), a plan that was developed collaboratively by the IMF and the Haitian government.

The Haitian government, with the support of the IMF, has sought to increase the independence of the central bank, the Bank of

[5] In a successful, small, open, developing-country economy, industry might account for 30 percent of GDP.

[6] IMF (2010, p. 6).

the Republic of Haiti (BRH), so as to better control inflation, primarily by reducing and eventually ceasing to provide direct financing to the government to cover budgetary shortfalls. The BRH has committed to attempt to slow rates of inflation by keeping increases in base money below growth in nominal GDP, informing market participants of changes in monetary aggregates by providing monetary data on a monthly basis, and smoothing fluctuations in the exchange rate.

The BRH's performance in terms of monetary policy has been satisfactory. Inflation moderated following the signing of the PRGF and fell sharply in 2009 from 2008 levels. The BRH has made interest rates more market-based by permitting a broader set of private-sector participants to bid on BRH bonds, including permitting individuals to purchase bonds through registered brokers. The BRH has also done a better job of publishing information on monetary developments.

In the aftermath of the earthquake, the government, in conjunction with the IMF, has revised monetary policy to take account of the effects of the earthquake. Monetary policy has been relaxed slightly. Although the government is seeking to keep inflation below 10 percent per year, it is cognizant that the influx of foreign assistance may contribute to higher inflation rates than would otherwise be the case as dollars are converted into gourdes for spending on the domestic economy. Following the earthquake, the BRH and the IMF agreed that monetary policy would be run so as to create conditions for credit expansion. Under the PRGF, base money was to grow at a rate slower than nominal GDP. In the revised plan, the real monetary base will be permitted to grow at the same pace as real GDP. The BRH will try to avoid funding the budget deficit, but, if commitments for foreign assistance fail to materialize in a timely manner, the BRH may provide bridge finance, as it did in 2009.[7]

Exchange-Rate Policy

Because Haiti is so poor, many Haitians spend more than half their incomes on food. However, more than half of all food consumed in Haiti is imported. When prices of food on world markets rise, as they

---

[7] Republic of Haiti (2010a).

did in 2008, these price increases feed directly into domestic inflation. In addition, Haiti relies on refined oil products for virtually all of its energy needs aside from domestically produced charcoal, the fuel with which most Haitian households cook. The large increases in world market prices for oil were another factor causing the surge in inflation in 2008. In fact, the acceleration in inflation in Haiti in 2008 was solely due to higher prices for food and oil; domestic factors were driving inflation down. Conversely, the sharp fall in inflation in Haiti in 2009 was triggered by falling world market prices for oil and food. Because imported goods figure so importantly in consumer expenditures, Haiti's exchange rate is an important determinant of inflation. When the gourde depreciates against the dollar, it has immediate inflationary consequences.

The exchange rate also plays a key role in domestic financial markets. The Haitian economy is heavily dollarized: Seventy-five percent of bank assets and 55 percent of bank liabilities are denominated in dollars. Shifts in the exchange rate have a substantial effect on financial holdings: During periods of sharp declines in the value of the gourde, financial assets and liabilities shift into dollars, exacerbating downward pressures on the exchange rate.

Because of the key role the exchange rate vis-à-vis the dollar plays in determining consumer price inflation and in financial markets, one of the BRH's primary responsibilities is exchange-rate policy. Currently, the BRH focuses on smoothing excessive volatility while allowing the exchange rate to adjust to help absorb shocks.

Despite the official policy of a flexible exchange rate, because the economy is so heavily dollarized, the BRH faces financial pressures to keep the exchange rate steady in nominal terms. This frequently entails setting interest rates on gourde assets substantially higher than on dollar assets. As a result, Haitian banks prefer to lend to the BRH at these rates rather than lend to the private sector. The private sector often turns to borrowing in dollars so as to benefit from lower dollar interest rates. As a consequence, Haiti reaps the worst of both worlds: high domestic interest rates on gourdes and substantial exchange-rate risk for Haitian companies because of their debts in dollars.

Fiscal Policy

Taxes. Even compared to countries with similar per capita incomes to Haiti's, tax revenues take a modest share of GDP: Total tax revenues ran 10.6 and 10.7 percent of Haiti's GDP in 2007 and 2008, respectively. Of these totals, revenues from customs were equivalent to 3.1 percentage points of GDP. However, a number of institutions—for example, some NGOs—receive customs exemptions. Consequently, customs revenues are lower than the volume of imports entering Haiti would suggest. In addition to customs, important domestic taxes include excise taxes on fuels and telecommunications. These taxes tend to be regressive, as they are levied on items that almost all Haitian households, poor and rich alike, purchase directly or indirectly. Haiti also levies a value-added tax (VAT) of 10 percent, collected from importers and by the larger local companies. It is another important source of revenue.

The Haitian government also levies a 30-percent corporate income tax, a 6-percent social security tax, and a 3-percent health-insurance tax on wages from larger businesses; a business-license tax based on turnover; a payroll tax of 2 percent; property taxes; and capital-gains taxes.[8] Collecting these taxes is challenging and tax evasion common. Consequently, many of these taxes do not generate much in the way of revenues. Only 1.8 percent of government revenues derive from taxes on income, profits, or capital. As these taxes would be paid by wealthier Haitians, the failure to collect these taxes shifts the overall tax burden toward the poor.

Because revenues are so heavily geared toward customs and excise taxes, shifts in the value of trade or sales volumes have very substantial effects on total tax revenues. Taxes fell sharply in real terms in 2009 as international commodity prices dropped, reducing the nominal value of imports and the tax take.

In the GPRSP, the Haitian government committed itself to raising tax revenues as a share of GDP. It proposes to do so by improving the tax administration, most notably by reducing corruption, reducing or eliminating tax exemptions, and improving the coverage of eco-

---

[8] World Bank (undated [d]).

nomic activities in rural areas in the tax system. A key measure is to strengthen customs control, especially along the land border with the Dominican Republic and at the provincial ports. The government, with the help of the donor community, has installed a computerized data-collection system in five provincial ports and along the border with the Dominican Republic. The government also has committed to adjusting tax schedules so as to take account of the effects of inflation on revenues in real terms, correcting the distortions induced by certain taxes, and readjusting rates deemed too low (for example, turnover-tax rates) or too high (those for registering property). To improve revenue collection, information is now being collected on all taxpayers in a computerized central taxpayer file. The government is also now adjusting prices for refined petroleum products in line with the cost of purchasing the products. This has been unpopular because motorists, an influential political constituency, prefer controlled prices.

The earthquake completely disrupted tax collections. It destroyed the Ministry of Economy and Finance, disrupted tax-collection systems, and halted imports into and garment exports from Port-au-Prince. About 85 percent of all tax revenues are collected in or from Port-au-Prince. According to the Haitian government and the IMF, tax revenues for 2009–2010 are now projected to run less than half what had been forecast in the budget. The government has not increased projected current budgeted expenditures, but, without budget support from donors, the projected decline in tax revenues would expand the deficit by roughly 18 billion gourdes.

Expenditures. Total government expenditures in 2007 and 2008 ran 15.6 and 18.2 percent of GDP, respectively, of which 7 and 7.5 percentage points of GDP, respectively, were accounted for by capital spending. In general, government revenues cover only current expenditures; donors fund almost all of the Haitian government's capital expenditures. Wages and subsidies account for a large share of current expenditures. In 2008, the Haitian government's wage bill ran 4.7 percent of GDP compared to total current government expenditures of 10.7 percentage points of GDP.[9] Transfers and subsidies ran 2 percent-

---

[9] IMF (2010, p. 17).

age points of GDP in 2009, of which 1.6 percentage points of GDP (13 percent of current government spending) went to Électricité d'Haïti (EdH), the electricity parastatal,[10] to make up for electricity tariffs set below the cost of power and nonpayment. Subsidies for electricity have become a major fiscal burden. Subsidies rose during a period when service deteriorated. The Haitian government also provides guarantees to EdH to facilitate its purchases of fuel. Combined, government salaries and subsidies for electricity accounted for more than half of current government expenditures in 2009. Haiti's government budget is heavily weighted toward administrative costs and subsidies.

Foreign donors, government and private, fund a large share of services, such as education and health care, which are usually provided by governments, but that, in Haiti, are largely provided through foreign and local NGOs. Private providers teach four-fifths or more of students in primary and secondary schools and provide most health services. On average, governments of developing countries spend about 10.4 percent of GDP on education (4.2 percent), health care (2.6 percent), and general administration (3.6 percent).[11] In contrast, in the period from 2005 to 2007, the Haitian government spent, on average, 2.4 percent and 1.4 percent of GDP on education and health care, respectively, roughly half the average for developing countries.[12] In light of the low level of public services provided by the government in Haiti, the figures for ongoing government expenditures are not as small relative to other developing countries as they may seem at first glance.

The Haitian government has received fewer funds from donors for budget support than it would like, in part because of donors' concerns about the extent and efficacy of Haitian government spending. In addition to its modest role in providing education and health care, the Haitian government has a difficult time accounting for the activi-

---

[10] An entity that is quasi-governmental—that is, at least partly (if not entirely) owned by the government.

[11] Dobbins, Jones, et al. (2007, p. 157).

[12] This was a substantial increase from levels in 2002–2004, when government spending on education and health averaged 1.6 percent and 0.7 percent of GDP, respectively.

ties of some government employees. It does not have a complete census of these staff nor detailed job descriptions for them.

The GPRSP commits the Haitian government to shift expenditures from subsidies and transfers toward more public investment and greater spending on education and primary health care. The *Action Plan for National Recovery and Development of Haiti* reiterates the Haitian government's commitment to shifting expenditures to those areas. Both the international community and the Haitian government have focused on improving tax collection and financial management. The government has improved oversight by consolidating internal controls through a financial management information system (FMIS). The FMIS has helped improve budget preparation, provide better budgetary information, improve budget execution, and monitor and control spending. It has also helped improve public procurement. The Haitian government has committed to and met the goals of approving the budget before the start of the fiscal year; publishing information on budget execution on a monthly basis; and limiting discretionary spending through ministerial current accounts to less than 10 percent of nonwage spending in the budget. It has also committed to verifying civil service employment based on attendance lists so as to eliminate ghost workers, although this has reportedly not yet been achieved.

Budget Balance. In the past, budget deficits were a major cause of inflation in Haiti, as the central bank was pressed to finance them by printing money. Under the new monetary policy framework, monetizing budget deficits has become less of a threat. Now the government is constrained to finance its current expenditures. In some instances, the government has resorted to wage arrears when revenues have been insufficient to finance current expenditures. This has been a periodic problem since the earthquake. As noted earlier, the BRH can also still offer temporary bridge financing to the government.

On a consolidated basis, the Haitian government continues to run deficits. Capital expenditures had often been financed by bilateral donors or loans from the international development banks. Since the earthquake, the international community has committed to financing capital expenditures through grants.

Government Debt. Haiti has been granted considerable debt relief: Both the World Bank and the IDB have written off their loans to Haiti. Despite the large debt write-offs, total public debt still ran 23.2 percent of GDP in 2009. Haiti added to its debt in 2009 by borrowing from Venezuela, albeit at concessional rates. This and some other debt owed private creditors have not been forgiven. However, for the immediate future, debt as a share of GDP does not appear problematic. The bigger challenge is generating sufficient export revenues to finance this debt. Because exports constitute such a small share of GDP and debt is primarily financed from external sources, the Haitian government may face difficulties in financing its debt if foreign exchange earnings fall, even by small amounts.

Financial-Sector Policies

Haiti had a small but well-capitalized banking sector that served the formal economy before the earthquake. As the economy grew from 2002 to 2009, the financial sector grew rapidly. However, in 2007, lending to the private sector still ran less than 15 percent of GDP, of which more than half was in dollars.

The earthquake had a devastating effect on the financial sector. Citibank's building was totally destroyed; five employees were killed. Citibank is one of the major banks in the country. Banking operations for the sector as a whole have recommenced, but a number of borrowers have suffered devastating losses from the earthquake. Consequently, a number of bank assets are heavily impaired. If borrowers were uninsured, which is probably the case in most instances, foreign donors may have to step in and finance the recapitalization of the banking sector. Foreign-owned banks should be able to rely on their parent companies to recapitalize.

Money transfer operations are the most widespread, competitive part of the financial sector. Demand is strong as the Haitian diaspora transfers funds to family and friends throughout the country. Money transfer operations quickly returned to service following the earthquake. The sector is a mixture of private and nonprofit. Western Union is active. Fonkoze, a subsidiary of Bangladesh's microfinance pioneer, Grameen Bank, also handles money transfers.

Microlending is the third component of the financial sector. It serves 200,000 families and businesses and is well entrenched. For example, Fonkoze has been in Haiti for 15 years. It has an extensive branch network of 38 banks and a client base of 50,000 borrowers. Fonkoze has been able to restore operations since the earthquake.

In contrast to a number of other areas, financial regulation functions fairly well in Haiti. The BRH regulates the formal banking sector. Money transfer operations are generally unregulated, as are microfinance operations. However, these institutions have performed well. The major transfer operators have an excellent record of delivering money. The microlending operations have maintained solvency. Although the BRH does not regulate their activities, both money transfer points and microfinance institutions have to register with the government.

Like the rest of the Haitian economy, the financial sector has been stunted. Solvent demand for credit and other financial services has been low because sectors that demand credit in more-successful economies, such as construction, manufacturing, and wholesaling, have been unable to thrive in Haiti due to political turmoil, lack of security, and the poor business environment. Not surprisingly, the only part of the financial sector that has done well in the past few decades has been money transfer operations. They have served the needs of Haiti's largest export: people.

Policies to Improve the Business Environment

In its GPRSP, the Haitian government has committed itself to reducing the time it takes to register a business or property and to obtain permits. Reducing the time spent to register a business or property will entail eliminating some of the steps in the process and accelerating other processes; in most instances, reducing transaction times should also be accompanied by reducing charges. The proposed changes entail changes in laws, which must be passed by Parliament. These changes have been slow to take place.

Recommendations

The Haitian economy needs to enjoy a period of sustained, steady growth. Without such a period, Haitians will remain mired in poverty, with all of its accompanying ills. To generate growth, Haiti will have to sustain macroeconomic stability, improve the environment for business, and capitalize on favorable treatment it has been granted by the international community. With the adoption of the HOPE II Act by the U.S. government, Haiti enjoys highly favorable access to the U.S. market for clothing. Some of Haiti's best prospects for growth are to attract foreign and domestic investment to the garment industry. Haiti has too many people engaged in agriculture. The country is heavily populated, and more land is cultivated than is ecologically sustainable. In contrast, labor-intensive industries, such as garment manufacturing, provide an attractive source of jobs and income, especially given Haiti's competitive, low-cost labor force. However, to take advantage of the opportunities in labor-intensive exports, the Haitian government, in conjunction with the international community, should implement the recommendations set forth in this section.

Assess Whether to Replace the Gourde with the U.S. Dollar

The Haitian government, in conjunction with the BRH and the IMF, should conduct a detailed review of the advantages and disadvantages of replacing the gourde with the U.S. dollar. A number of small, open economies that enjoy very large inflows of remittances and trade predominantly with one major trading partner have chosen to adopt the currency of that partner. For example, El Salvador and Ecuador have adopted the U.S. dollar, and Kosovo and Montenegro have adopted the euro. Adopting a foreign currency eases the day-to-day strains on the central bank by eliminating the need to manage the exchange rate or monetary policy. It also helps control inflation. The advantage of a domestic currency—namely, the ability to let the exchange rate adjust in response to changes in economic conditions—is much less valuable for small, open economies, such as Haiti's, in which changes in exchange rates feed directly into domestic inflation. Problems of exchange-rate instability are exacerbated when residents calculate prices and keep most assets in foreign currency. Moreover, in countries with a limited pool of highly trained economists on which to draw, adopting a foreign currency frees up scarce talent to work in the Ministry of Economy and Finance or elsewhere in government or in the financial sector. For these reasons, Haiti might benefit from following El Salvador in adopting the dollar. However, the Haitian government would be able to replace the gourde with the dollar only after an extensive national discussion. During our consultations, reactions in Haiti to this idea were negative, as respondents argued that it would be unpopular politically. Elsewhere, use of a foreign currency as the local currency has often been popular.

Streamline the Tax System

In light of the earthquake and a substantial influx of donor funds planned for the next few years, the government of Haiti should delay increasing the share of GDP taken in taxes until the domestic economy is on a more solid footing. *However, the Haitian government should use this period to streamline the tax system by shifting toward electronic verification and eliminating provisions that encumber economic growth, such as fees charged to street vendors and revenue taxes.* First and foremost, this should involve completely implementing the new customs-management system.

As part of streamlining the tax system, the Haitian government should eliminate tax exemptions, including those currently provided NGOs. The provision of exemptions, including to the international donor community, has detrimental consequences for tax collection and for ensuring that all players in product markets enjoy a level playing field. Tariff exemptions for imported vehicles have distorted the market for motor vehicles. Exemptions to turnover taxes for NGOs deprive the government of revenues from the provision of services. These distortions should be eliminated.

Haiti has one of the most inequitable distributions of income in the world. *Once the economy shows signs of recovery, the Haitian government should shift the burden of taxes to higher-income groups by levying higher property taxes on real estate.* It should also levy higher taxes on purchases or imports of automobiles and light trucks.

Improve the Environment for Business

The Haitian government should move quickly to eliminate unnecessary procedures involved in registering businesses and property and reduce the cost and length of time needed to complete the remaining steps. For example, the Haitian government should implement "one-stop" registration of businesses. It should eliminate mandatory fees and open up competition for the provision of services by notary publics. It should also eliminate charges associated with repossessing collateral.

CHAPTER SEVEN

Housing and Infrastructure

The Challenges

The earthquake has had a devastating effect on houses and apartment buildings in Haiti. Although the tent cities have been an effective stopgap measure, the most important reconstruction challenge for Haiti and the international community is to provide housing for the displaced that will shelter Haitians from tropical storms and hurricanes in this and coming years.

In addition to housing, Haiti and the international community will need to reconstruct and improve Haiti's infrastructure (roads, ports, airports, electric-power system, water, and sewage), if Haiti is to enjoy sustained economic growth and the health and well-being of its citizens are to improve. However, expanding infrastructure is not just a question of building new highways and power plants. The Haitian government and donors must also set up systems for maintaining infrastructure once built and, as importantly, ensure that utilities charge and collect enough revenues to fully cover the costs of services, such as electricity, water, and sewage, that they provide. In many respects, the current parlous state of Haiti's infrastructure has more to do with the failure to ensure that infrastructure is well maintained and operated than to lack of money for the construction of new projects.

The GPRSP lays out a goal of slowing the influx of Haitians from rural areas into Port-au-Prince and Haiti's smaller cities. If this goal is to be achieved, incomes in rural communities will need to rise and the cost of living relative to Port-au-Prince and other coastal cities will have to fall. In a small, open economy, such as Haiti's, the cost of importing and exporting goods is a major determinant of the cost of living and export competitiveness. For rural areas to thrive, residents and businesses need to be able to procure and ship products cheaply and quickly. This will entail building and maintaining all-weather roads to rural communities. Businesses will also need reliable access to electricity. Without reliable electricity, sectors in rural areas, such as food processing, assembly plants, and hotels, will not be able to flourish.

In this chapter, we focus on housing, roads, seaports and airports, electric power, water, sewage, and housing. For reasons of space and the absence of major policy issues, we do not discuss reconstructing public buildings. We see this task as relatively straightforward compared to building and operating other sorts of infrastructure. We also do not believe that rebuilding ministerial buildings is as important as providing functional temporary facilities from which ministries can operate while housing, ports, and roads are being reconstructed. In our view, Haiti and the Haitian government would be better served by focusing on improving the lot of the citizens than reconstructing permanent public buildings.

We also do not include telecommunications in our discussion of utilities. With the introduction of a competitive market for cellular telephone services in Haiti, cell-phone access and coverage are expanding rapidly. As in other developing countries, the market appears to be addressing demand for these services quickly and more efficiently than the state-owned telecommunication utility. In recognition of the rapid growth in this sector, the government is privatizing the state-owned telecommunication company.

Housing

Most households in Haiti, including those in Port-au-Prince and the coastal cities, construct their own homes. As shown by the destruction caused by the earthquake, many of these homes were not built to withstand natural disasters. Reinforcement, especially the use of steel reinforcement bars in concrete buildings, was inadequate. Concrete blocks, bricks, and cement were often of poor quality.

In light of these structural deficiencies, it is not surprising that, in the aftermath of the earthquake, Haiti's most pressing current problem is housing. According to the PDNA, about 105,000 homes were totally destroyed and more than 208,000 were damaged by the earthquake; 1.3 million Haitians had to move into temporary shelters.[1] Housing suffered the most damage of any sector from the earthquake.

For housing to be reconstructed, sites have to be cleared. The rate at which rubble is being removed has been very slow: Only a small fraction of destroyed buildings have been torn down and sites cleared. Donors and the Haitian government have been at fault. Haitians whom donors have hired to clear rubble have not been equipped with gloves, boots, or hard hats. Heavy equipment has been in short supply. Haitian government customs officials have reportedly blocked the import of heavy equipment at the border with the Dominican Republic.[2] The government has also not yet designated sufficient space on which to dump rubble. Unless rubble is cleared expeditiously, hundreds of thousands of Haitians will still be in tent camps during the 2011 hurricane season.

Roads

The limited number of roads and their poor condition are major impediments to economic growth, especially in rural areas. Despite its long seacoast, 80 percent of Haiti's people and goods move by road. Yet Haiti has a very small road network: only 3,400 kilometers of roads, of which less than 800 kilometers are paved (24 percent of the network). Many rural communities lack access to improved roads; goods and people move along dirt tracks. Because of Haiti's mountainous terrain, heavy rainfall, and poor track record on maintenance, even those roads that have been improved often become impassable as sections are washed out during the rainy season. Due to lack of maintenance, the size of the officially registered tertiary network has fallen by more than half between 1991 and 2004.[3] More than 70 percent of roads remain in poor or very poor condition.

---

1 Republic of Haiti (2010a).

2 Johnson (2010).

3 World Bank (2008a).

Seaports and Airports

All the major towns situated along Haiti's coasts have seaports. However, most cargo is shipped through the ports of Port-au-Prince. Moreover, until recently, the state-owned port at Port-au-Prince had a monopoly on container traffic. The port was heavily damaged during the earthquake. The international community, especially the U.S. military, was able to rapidly repair and reopen the port.

The costs of shipping through Haiti's ports have imposed a major burden on Haitian consumers and businesses. Because imports play such an important role in consumption, investment, and business operations, the cost of imports is a key determinant of living standards and economic growth. Importing a container of goods is 35 percent more expensive in Haiti than the average for developed OECD countries and 4 percent more expensive than the average cost of importing a container in Latin America. Importing a container into Haiti also takes appreciably more time than the average for the OECD: 33 days compared to 11 days. These differences in costs and time reduce the standards of living of Haitians and make it more difficult for export businesses to compete. On a more positive note, the costs of exporting a container are lower in Haiti than the average for Latin America or for the OECD, primarily because Haiti imports more goods than it exports: Exporters are able to lease containers for much less money on the return because there is a surfeit of empty containers.[4]

Haiti's main airport at Port-au-Prince was also heavily damaged by the earthquake. It was reopened with the assistance of the U.S. military. Passengers are now processed in a temporary facility. Although the airport functions, the terminal building and other facilities will need to be repaired if Haiti is to attract foreign business travelers and tourists in the coming years.

Electricity

One of the greatest impediments to sustained economic growth in Haiti is the lack of access to uninterrupted supplies of electricity at competitive prices. Haiti has one of the lowest access rates to electricity

---

[4] World Bank (undated [b]).

in the world (12.5 percent of the population in 2005).[5] According to the household living-conditions survey report for 2003, only 11 percent of rural households have access to electricity, compared to 70 percent of the wealthiest quintile.[6]

With the assistance of donors, the Haitian government has been investing in electric-power generating capacity. Between 2004 and 2009, three new thermal-power plants were constructed and brought into service in Port-au-Prince, Cap Haïtien, and Gonaïves, each with a capacity of 30 megawatts.

The primary challenge facing Haiti's state-owned utility, EdH, is covering costs. Electricity tariffs have been set below full cost-recovery levels. As of mid-2009, the government charged only 6.5 gourdes ($0.163) per kilowatt-hour for power that cost 13 gourdes ($0.325) per kilowatt-hour to generate. As a consequence, EdH loses substantial amounts of money. Covering these losses has become a major item in Haiti's national budget. The high cost of power in Haiti stems from the use of diesel fuel to power generating plants; every generating plant except one runs solely on diesel fuel. In addition, the power company gets paid for only about 50 percent of the electricity it delivers because of theft and nonpayment by users. Consequently, revenue shortfalls are even greater than suggested by the difference between costs and rates. Financial problems in the electric-power sector are so severe that, in 2009, two of Haiti's new generators stopped operating because funds to purchase fuel ran out.

Water and Sewage

Haiti also lags in providing water and sewage services. Only 54 percent of the population has access to sources of improved water, compared to 91 percent of citizens in the rest of Latin America and the Caribbean. Only 30 percent of the population has access to improved sewage, compared to 77 percent of the people in the region.[7] In addition to lack of coverage, especially for the rural population, existing water and

---

5 World Bank (2008a).

6 IHSI (2005).

7 World Bank (2009c).

sewage systems did not function well before the earthquake. Staff did not always fulfill their duties correctly, and maintenance was shortchanged. Fortunately, the earthquake does not appear to have inflicted major damage on existing water and sewage systems.

Appraisal of Plans and Initiatives for Addressing the Challenges

Housing

The Haitian government states that it wants to channel reconstruction so that it is consistent with land-use plans for Port-au-Prince and other cities. It also wants to better use available land. It has charged municipalities with ensuring that reconstruction is consistent with their land-use plans. However, in recognition of the limitations on qualified staff and capacity to implement policies, the government has noted that it will need technical assistance and human and material resources from donors to train staff and implement a system for monitoring construction.[8]

The Haitian government has promised to use its power of eminent domain to intervene in land use. The Haitian government issued a decree on March 19, 2010, allowing municipalities to develop new urban plans and to relocate families affected by the earthquake to available land. The Haitian authorities have stated that they plan to both sell state-owned land and, where necessary, purchase privately held land to rationalize holdings and use of urban land. Sales and purchases are to be at market values. However, this change has not yet been implemented. In light of the potential opposition, it is likely to be delayed.

Two of the key problems that emerged in the aftermath of the earthquake were lax enforcement and, in some instances, the absence of building codes and standards. Reconstructing privately owned buildings and residences will require a level of monitoring that goes well beyond what was done in the past. Here, too, the Haitian govern-

---

8 Republic of Haiti (2010a, p. 12).

ment is relying on the municipalities. However, donors will likely need to play a major role in training and paying personnel and providing equipment and supervision.

Before housing can begin to be reconstructed, rubble has to be cleared and dumped at a site. The Haitian government hopes to find areas where steel reinforcement bars can be removed and rubble can be pounded into aggregate and reused in road construction or for fill. Because of very high population densities in Port-au-Prince and surrounding areas, the government has had difficulty in finding sites, even on the outskirts of the capital.

Roads

The Haitian government and the international donor community have made road construction a development priority. Programs have focused on connecting the major cities and towns with all-weather trunk roads and providing road access to rural communities. The government has plans to add an additional 600 kilometers of primary and secondary roads to ensure that all parts of the country are linked by paved roads.[9] The World Bank, the French government, and other donors have provided the initial funds for this program.

The Haitian government and a group of donors comprised of the World Bank, the United Nations International Strategy for Disaster Reduction (ISDR), Australia, Canada, Denmark, the EU, Finland, France, Germany, Italy, Japan, Luxembourg, Norway, Spain, Sweden, Switzerland, and the United Kingdom have drawn up a priority investment program aimed at rehabilitating 600 kilometers of roads (one-quarter of the system) over the period 2006–2011. These donors and the Haitian government have coordinated their efforts through a body set up specifically for transportation projects, the Table Sectorielle Transport. The Table Sectorielle Transport has worked effectively to coordinate donor-funded projects and provide transportation policy recommendations to the government of Haiti.[10]

---

[9] Republic of Haiti (2010a, p. 14).

[10] World Bank (2008b).

The World Bank has been one of the leading donors in the transport sector through the International Development Agency (IDA), its arm for providing grant aid and low-cost loans to the least developed countries. The EU and the IDB have also been important donors. The Haitian government has set priorities for investment by preparing a strategy for the transport sector for 2006–2011 with support from the World Bank. Haiti also has a national intermodal transport plan that the EU has supported.

Since 2004, the Haitian government has adopted a number of measures to strengthen the road maintenance system. With donor support, especially from the World Bank, the Haitian government has set up the Road Maintenance Fund (Fonds d'Entretien Routier, or FER). FER has developed capacity to implement maintenance projects, financing routine and emergency road repairs. Revenues come from the proceeds of a gasoline tax that is collected and transferred to FER by the Ministry of Economy and Finance.[11] Despite these institutional improvements, FER has not ensured that roads are maintained. The organization has had difficulty in laying out a program of scheduled maintenance, contracting with companies to repair roads, and ensuring that contracted repairs have been completed in a satisfactory manner.

Despite the importance ascribed to improving the road network, the record concerning foreign assistance in this sector is mixed.[12] Between 2004 and 2008, Haiti received roughly $2 billion in foreign aid, of which about one-quarter went to the transport sector, primarily roads and ports. Despite the creation of FER, the Haitian government still does not have a strong maintenance plan, nor has it implemented those maintenance plans upon which it has agreed. Several projects have been built but then deteriorated because of lack of maintenance. The four major storms that hit Haiti in 2008 washed out a number of sections of major roads and bridges. Where roads and bridges had been properly maintained, damage from hurricanes and tropical storms was substantially less than on stretches of roads where mainte-

---

[11] World Bank (2008b).

[12] World Bank (2008a).

nance had been less satisfactory. Roads are also prone to deterioration because the government does not adequately enforce standards for road construction.

In addition to problems with maintenance, the Haitian government has had difficulties in planning the road network, implementing plans, contracting, and conducting physical audits to ensure that contracted work has been completed as promised.

Seaports and Airports

The Haitian government has made moves toward reducing the costs and time involved in importing and exporting containers of goods. International assistance has been used to buy out surplus workers at the state-owned port in Port-au-Prince. Having fewer staff has resulted in more-rapid movement of goods. The government has also made some moves toward more competition by promising to permit private investors to operate container terminals. However, government officials have argued that the state-owned port needs more time to modernize before it is exposed to the full force of competition, so private container terminals have faced constraints on their operations.[13]

The earthquake closed the port of Port-au-Prince for a period. During this time, the government of Haiti relaxed, but did not repeal, restrictions on importing containers through other ports. The increased competition has resulted in much more rapid movement of goods during humanitarian relief at lower cost.

The Haitian government would like to expand and modernize port capacity. In particular, it would like to reduce the role of the current port of Port-au-Prince by constructing new facilities, including a terminal for large container ships, away from the current location of the port. It also hopes to build two other deep-water ports, at Cap Haïtien and Gonaïves.[14]

The Haitian government has made a commitment to make greater use of public-private partnerships for investments in infrastructure.[15] It

---

[13] Discussions with Haitian government officials, Port-au-Prince, April 14, 2010.

[14] Republic of Haiti (2010a, p. 15).

[15] Republic of Haiti (2010a, p. 26).

has stated that it will encourage build-operate-transfer (BOT) projects for ports, electric power, and other areas of infrastructure. However, the private sector's willingness to invest in BOT port projects depends on firms' ability to levy charges that will provide a positive rate of return and to operate ports in a competitive fashion. The government of Haiti will need to ensure that investors can operate their ports efficiently and profitably. For its part, the government of Haiti needs to protect itself by ensuring that the private-sector operators, not it, bear the risk of constructing and managing the facility in a profitable manner.

In its *Action Plan for National Recovery and Development of Haiti*, the Haitian government calls for repairing and extending Haiti's sole international airport at Port-au-Prince and building two new international airports, one at Les Cayes and the other at Cap Haïtien. Repairs and the new airports are to be conducted on a BOT basis.

Although the Port-au-Prince airport should be attractive to a private-sector partner, the other proposed airports would probably have to be developed sequentially and after the Port-au-Prince airport has been reconstructed. They will probably also have to be built in tandem with resorts or manufacturing plants to ensure that they will enjoy enough traffic to make the investment worthwhile.

Electricity

The *Action Plan for National Recovery and Development of Haiti* focuses on (1) expanding generating capacity, (2) improving the transmission system in Port-au-Prince and along the Léogâne/Petit-Goâve axis, and (3) only after these steps are taken, expanding the distribution network. The plan also mentions that significant efforts need to be made to improve the management of the distribution system. However, there is little mention of electricity-tariff reform and no plan for improving payment discipline. There is also no mention of what the private sector might do in this area.

Under the PRGF with the IMF, Haiti's authorities committed to increasing electricity tariffs to cost-recovery levels by the end of September 2009, while protecting poor households. The government met the target of creating a tariff structure that would lead to full cost recovery by September 2009 and began to raise tariffs. However, increases have not yet reached full cost-recovery levels. In light of the earthquake, tariff increases have been pushed back again. If tariffs are increased to full cost-recovery levels, the government's large transfers to EdH for operating expenditures would end. However, the government has committed to still provide funds for investments to increase supply and reliability of service.

In addition to setting electric-power tariffs at levels below the cost of generating power, EdH has a poor record of collecting from users. Management does not closely track payments and does not move quickly to cut off deadbeats. Theft of power through illegal hookups is common; EdH does little to combat theft by cutting wires or protecting lines.

As noted earlier, Haiti's generators run on diesel fuel. Because of the high costs of diesel fuel, in the *Action Plan for National Reconstruction and Development of Haiti*, the government states that it would like to draw on hydroelectric, wind, and solar power and lower-cost sources of fossil fuels. Hydropower is very capital-intensive. Wind power is also capital-intensive and needs to have skilled technicians capable of keeping windmills operating. Solar power is more expensive than hydro or wind power and substantially more expensive than many sources of fossil fuels. Independent power producers would use residual fuel oil (bunker fuel) for their plants. This source of energy is substantially cheaper than diesel and could significantly reduce the cost of electricity. However, until consumers pay the full costs of power, goals for moving to other sources of electricity will not be grounded in reality.

Water and Sewage

Before the earthquake, the Haitian government laid out a strategy for expanding and improving access to water and sewage in the GPRSP. Its strategy focused on strengthening the technical capabilities of the water authorities and making them financially autonomous. The government planned to rehabilitate and expand coverage so that 60 percent of the population of Port-au-Prince and 73 percent of the population in other urban areas would have access to clean water. The entire plan was estimated to cost $400 million, of which $200 million has already been committed.

The government is planning major institutional changes, including replacing the local authorities currently in charge of water and sewage (Service National d'Eau Potable [SNEP], Centrale Autonome Métropolitaine d'Eau Potable [CAMEP], and Poste Communautaire d'Hygiène et d'Eau Potable [POCHEP]) with new regional water and sanitation offices. The new regional offices would have an obligation to provide service to current users and to expand the system to connect new users, especially shantytowns and low-income rural populations. They would also set up new water catchment areas and expand water- and waste-treatment facilities. The new entities may be managed by private operators.

A drinking-water and sanitation directorate is to be set up within the Ministry of Public Works, Transport and Communications and is to focus on regulating the sector. It will define policy on tariffs for water and sewage, set standards for water quality, and set conditions to be met by operators who bid to manage the systems.[16]

The government is also planning to introduce a pricing system for water and sewage that would generate sufficient revenue to cover operating costs and at least some of the costs of the investments made but that would also be structured so that lower-income users would pay lower prices.

Recommendations

Take Immediate Steps to Accelerate the Removal of Rubble

Unless rubble is removed from building sites, reconstruction of housing and businesses cannot proceed. *The Haitian government, in conjunction with the donor community, should accelerate the removal of rubble.* We believe that this is the single most important step toward reconstruction that the Haitian government and the donor community can take. Donors need to immediately make available adequate funds to hire Haitian companies to quickly remove all rubble. Donors, working together with the government, should take bids and select prime

[16] Republic of Haiti (2008, p. 47).

contractors, be they NGOs or private companies, to subcontract rubble removal by subcontractors or work crews, who should be responsible for individual sites. Donors should also encourage companies owning dump trucks to collaborate with rubble-removing crews to transport the rubble to disposal sites. The Haitian government needs to locate and ensure that there are sites prepared for disposing of rubble. It also needs to conduct physical and financial audits to ensure that rubble is properly removed.

Focus on Repairing and Maintaining Existing Roads

Developing capacity to maintain roads once built should be the top transport priority of the Haitian government and the international donor community. All new road construction in Haiti should be accompanied by a fully funded maintenance plan, and all road rebuilding and maintenance in Haiti should be channeled through the FER.

Remove Remaining Restrictions on the Operations of Private Container Ports

The Haitian government should aggressively seek to encourage private operators to develop ports, terminals, and airports in Haiti through BOT projects. However, the government should not guarantee revenues or rates of return, nor should it provide monopolistic franchises to operators.

Immediately Move to Raise Electric-Power Tariffs to Full Cost-Recovery Levels

The Haitian government should also separate distribution from the other operations of EdH. *Retail distribution operations should either be sold or contracted out to independent providers, be they cooperatives, municipal agencies, or private companies.* EdH should operate as a wholesaler, selling power to these groups. These groups should be responsible for the local distribution network, including collecting revenues from end users. Local distribution operators should be responsible for making payments to EdH for power consumed within their area. If payments are not made, power supplies should be cut to service areas. Because they are closer to the local community, have an incentive to collect payment, and have the flexibility to improve local distribution, local distribution companies are likely to greatly improve payment discipline and quality of service as they have elsewhere in the developing world.

The Haitian government should eliminate barriers to entry of independent power producers but should stipulate that producers' sales of power to EdH will be at the producers' risk; the Haitian government should not guarantee payments.

CHAPTER EIGHT

Education

The Challenges

Long-Standing Challenges

As the Haitian government reported in its PDNA, "(the) education system already presented deficiencies before the earthquake that made it unfit to contribute to socio-economic development."[1] Low quality, lack of access, and little oversight characterized the country's education sector. The state played a very limited role in providing and regulating schooling, a fact that contributed to an incoherent education system. Enrollment rates and levels of educational attainment were very low. About one-half of Haitian adults were illiterate;[2] according to the *World Development Indicators* database, the average adult has 2.8 years of schooling. About half of school-aged children were not in any form of school.[3] Although many children experienced *some* schooling in episodic spells, a large number did not obtain a complete basic education. According to the most-recent available longitudinal evidence, about 33 percent of children who attended school reached the fifth grade[4] and only 4 percent completed nine years of school and subsequently entered secondary education.[5] The problem was worse in rural areas,

---

1 Republic of Haiti (2010b).

2 Wolff (2008).

3 World Bank (undated [c]).

4 IDB (2010).

5 Salmi (1998).

where approximately three-quarters of children did not attend school,[6] even though almost all children (98 percent) lived within 10 kilometers of a primary school.[7] The condition of primary and secondary education in Haiti was, and remains, the worst of any country in the Americas.[8]

The most-pressing needs for the education system in Haiti are as follows:

- substantially *expanded access* to education—a task that would require the government to spend many times more than what it currently does on education over and above the costs of rebuilding the approximately 5,000 schools destroyed in the 2010 earthquake
- *improved quality* of education, which requires recruiting, educating, and training teachers in pedagogy; establishing a national curriculum and providing textbooks that align with content standards; and reducing the numbers of overage students by grade
- development of a system of *oversight* to ensure increased access and enforce improved measures of quality, including the establishment of a regulatory system to accredit and inspect both schools and teacher-training programs.

For decades, donors and the Haitian government have been aware of these needs and have attempted to address them. For example, Haiti's 1997 national education plan[9] set targets for improved quality and access in support of Education for All (EFA) goals,[10] which led to

---

6 IDB (2010).

7 IDB (2010).

8 Wolff (2008).

9 MENFP (1997).

10 EFA dates to the 1990 World Conference on Education for All, at which 155 countries committed to provide education for all children. Specific EFA goals were then set out at the Dakar World Education Forum in 2000. At a UN summit in 2000, the Millennium Development Goals (MDGs) stipulated that all boys and girls should complete a full cycle of primary education by 2015. The EFA goals encompass those MDGs that pertain to education, and the Fast Track Initiative seeks to aid developing countries in achieving the Millennium

increased public funding and a greater number of slots for students.[11] But, more than a decade later, enrollment still remained low, and the rates at which students repeat grades increased over time—partly a result of unstable economic conditions, frequent dropping in and out, failure to pass tests (resulting in retention within the grade level), and low attendance.[12] Meanwhile, the large majority of schools were not accredited, and most teachers were poorly trained.

Given the extremely poor condition of the education system, most donors focused on expanding and improving the formal basic education system. Generally speaking, a *formal basic education* in Haiti is organized into three periods over nine years—the first lasting about four years, a second period for two years, and a third (corresponding to U.S. grades 7–9) for three years. The third period is separated into two branches: one for general education and a second for technical or professional preparation. Beyond formal basic education, there is a three-year secondary-school system, in which students can choose between traditional, technical, and vocational schools.

There were about 160 institutions of higher education in Haiti prior to the earthquake, of which 14 were publicly run. Like primary education, the higher-education system was in very poor shape; the Ministry of Education and Training (Ministère de l'Education Nationale et de la Formation Professionnelle, or MENFP) itself concluded in 1997 that many universities operated as such only in name with no regard for providing a university-level education.[13]

Haiti is unusual in that private institutions dominate the education sector. Prior to the earthquake, 80 percent of Haitian students were enrolled in nonpublic schools.[14] According to the United Nations

---

Development/EFA goals. The Fast Track Initiative currently provides funds to 41 developing countries, including Haiti.

[11] Library of Congress (2006).

[12] Grade-level repetition is (imprecisely) estimated at 9 percent in 1985, 20 percent in 1997, and approximately 25 percent in 2008 (Hadjadj, 2000; Wolff, 2008).

[13] For example, in postearthquake focus groups, students reported serious breaches of quality, such as professors assessing fees to write theses for their students (INURED, 2010).

[14] World Bank (undated [c]).

Educational, Scientific and Cultural Organization (UNESCO), only four countries in the world exceed this rate of private-sector enrollment in primary education: Macau, Zimbabwe, Belize, and Aruba. Haitian private schools were largely unregulated: Only about 10 percent of primary schools and one-third of secondary schools were licensed.[15] The private sector greatly expanded in both higher and primary education over the course of the 1990s, accounting for most of the growth in the total number of school enrollments for that period of time.[16] Private schools were financed by a combination of parent fees and subsidies from organizations, such as churches, charities, and foreign-government aid. More than half of private schools were religiously affiliated (Protestant groups ran the largest share); church groups often operated rural schools.[17]

While public spending on education was about 2 percent of GDP prior to the earthquake, private spending comprised almost 7 percent of GDP—among the highest rates in the world.[18] Annual school fees at private schools were approximately $70 to $80 per child, which is equal to one-sixth of per capita GDP. This is especially striking when one considers that more than three-quarters of Haitians live on less than $2 per day.[19]

Food distribution was a crucial draw for student enrollment. Based on the most-recent evidence available, approximately one-third of private-school students depended on feeding programs.[20] Despite the pervasive problem of hunger in Haiti, less than one in five schools had a school canteen as of 1997.[21] Although the country had a national

---

[15] Salmi (1998).

[16] Hadjadj (2000); INURED (2010).

[17] Hadjadj (2000); telephone conversation with Haitian academic, May 2010.

[18] MENFP (2007, in Wolff, 2008).

[19] IHSI (2005).

[20] Salmi (1998).

[21] Hadjadj (2000).

school feeding program up until the earthquake, it was not sufficiently funded to reach all the children attending private and public schools.[22]

Low quality characterizes all but a small set of elite schools; most private schools were considered to be of lower quality than public schools.[23] One factor explaining this public-private gap is that public-school teachers earned approximately two to three times more than private-school teachers.[24] Public schools, for their part, were also typically of low quality; public-school teachers often endured delayed or, at times, no pay from the government—a phenomenon that gives the Haitian diaspora pause when considering returning to work in education in Haiti following the earthquake.[25]

In a nation that lacks a middle class, which would normally supply teachers, it is not surprising that teacher quality is extremely low. As of 1997, teacher training was provided by unsupervised, private training institutions.[26] Between 70 and 80 percent of teachers lacked accreditation from the MENFP, and one-quarter had an educational level less than the ninth grade.[27] Tests administered to a representative sample of 1,200 private- and public-school teachers in 1996 showed that one in three teachers did not know how to sequence words alphabetically; eight in ten could not use the passive verb form in French; and fewer than one in ten performed satisfactorily on fourth-grade mathematics standards.[28]

Consequences of the Earthquake

The 2008 storms and the 2010 earthquake greatly exacerbated the weaknesses already inherent in Haiti's education system. Approxi-

---

22 For example, the World Bank had assembled a multidonor fund that had garnered a little more than $1 million in donor funds as of 2004 for school funding (World Bank, 2004).

23 IDB (2010).

24 Wolff (2008).

25 Telephone conversation with Haitian academic, May 2010.

26 Wolff (2008).

27 IDB (2010).

28 Salmi (1998).

mately 40,000 school children and more than 1,000 teachers died in January 2010. An estimated 49,000 teachers out of an approximate total of 60,000 worked in earthquake-affected areas.[29] More than 80 percent of Port-au-Prince school buildings were destroyed.[30] The system of higher education was virtually obliterated. Since university buildings were concentrated in areas most affected by the earthquake, 87 percent of the institutions of higher education were damaged or destroyed.[31] The building that housed the MENFP itself collapsed.

Formal schooling virtually ceased in the first months after the earthquake. The UN World Food Programme began providing food to children at school sites as of March 2010, with a plan to scale up to serve approximately 150 schools and 800,000 children.[32] Some schools first began to reopen for pupil instruction in April 2010.

Haiti was scheduled to sign a grant agreement in the week of the earthquake that would release $22 million into the Fast Track Initiative's (FTI) Catalytic Fund, a trust fund supervised by the World Bank.[33] Due to the earthquake, the originally planned uses for the funds have been shifted to a school resumption plan for the 2009–2010 year ($15 million), school feeding programs ($5 million), a UNESCO postdisaster teacher-training program ($1 million), and the purchase of emergency equipment.[34] As of this writing, the Catalytic Fund and an $80 million pledge from the IDB are the only two firm, education-specific commitments to rebuilding the education sector, although a number of countries have made pledges for Haitian reconstruction that have not yet been allocated to specific sectors.

The postearthquake education "cluster" for coordination of humanitarian aid (organized by the UN Office for the Coordination of Humanitarian Affairs) has been working on a host of short-term

---

29 Global Education Cluster (2010).

30 MENFP (2010a).

31 INURED (2010).

32 World Food Programme (2010).

33 Telephone conversation with representative of a multilateral organization, May 2010.

34 Catalytic Fund (2010).

issues to resume education. As a temporary means to restart schooling, the MENFP proposed, in April 2010, a five-month support program that will provide funds to nonpublic preschool through secondary schools in earthquake-affected areas of the country.[35] Ninety percent of the funds given to a school are to be used as a one-time payment to teachers (at no established salary schedule) for the duration of the 2009–2010 school year. Schools that receive the five-month grant may still assess fees from families, but the fees are expected to be lower than pre-earthquake rates, although there is no enforcement mechanism to ensure this. To implement the school resumption policy, the MENFP must first identify eligible schools for the funds: nonpublic schools that are ready to reopen, that have bank accounts to receive wired grant monies, and that can recruit a sufficient number of teachers.

The short-term payment to private schools, which indirectly pays for or at least reduces school fees, is one element of the action plan presented at the international donor conference held in New York on March 31, 2010.[36] With an 18-month horizon, the action plan focused on activities to facilitate the near-term resumption of schooling. Other activities in the action plan include the establishment of approximately 4,000 provisional school shelters and the supply of food to schools, both of which are ongoing.

Appraisal of Plans and Initiatives for Addressing the Challenges

Plans and Initiatives Before the Earthquake

In response to Haiti's pressing educational needs, international donor organizations have typically funded projects to fill gaps in service delivery, with the broad goal of meeting EFA universal basic-education targets. A UNESCO 2000 estimate placed collective donor giving to edu-

---

[35] Funding for resumption of at least some private schooling comes from $15 million of the $22 million in the Catalytic Fund and an additional $3 million from the IDB (MENFP, 2010a).

[36] Republic of Haiti (2010b).

cation at approximately $18 million per year (or $23 million in 2010 dollars) during the period of 1990–1999. At the time of the January 2010 earthquake, some donors were still working to provide emergency school relief to repair damage from the 2008 storms in Haiti.[37]

The turnover in Haiti's government leadership has made sustained education reform difficult and contributed to duplication in donor efforts. Between 1980 and 2000, there were 23 education ministers serving in 13 Haitian governments.[38] The succession of education ministers yielded plans and reforms that usually did not last from one administration to the next. Compounding the problem is the fact that Haiti lacks a precedent for an overarching education governance system; at no point in its history as an independent country has Haiti had a universal system of education for its children. Governmental reforms in the 1980s and 1990s did establish a relatively uniform structure for education and a system of national tests administered at those schools that are accredited, but schools are not obligated to operate by these rules. Since the vast majority of schools, including those in higher education, are unaccredited and private, the education "system" effectively consists of ad hoc decisions made by individual schools.

Despite these challenges, donors have attempted to coordinate their education activities in Haiti. Starting in 2003, UNESCO led a sectoral education group (groupe sectorielle de l'éducation) that met on a monthly basis and consisted of the main education actors in Haiti: a representative from the MENFP, representatives of assistance agencies from Canada (Canadian International Development Agency, or CIDA), Spain (Agencia Española de Cooperación Internacional para el Desarrollo, or AECID), France (Agence Française de Développement, or AFD), the EU, the United Nations Children's Fund (UNICEF), the World Bank, and the United States (USAID).[39] The donors in the

---

[37] For example, the World Bank had begun a $5 million project in 2009 to restore access to damaged public schools and to disseminate safe school construction standards (World Bank, 2009d).

[38] Hadjadj (2000).

[39] Telephone conversation with representative of donor organization 1, May 2010. The IDB observed but was not a member of the EFA/FTI group (IDB, 2010).

Haiti sectoral education group also belong to the set of 18 donors to FTI, which began in 2002 and helps developing countries to achieve the MDG that, by 2015, all children should complete a full course of basic formal education. The sectoral education group helped the Haitian government join FTI, which became the dominant framework for education reform after 2007 in Haiti.

Revised Plans

In consultation with the MENFP, donors are now debating two distinct approaches to restructuring education. However, absent firm commitments from the donor community to fund comprehensive long-term education building, it will be difficult for the MENFP to select a preferred means for redesigning the system. Nevertheless, the MENFP and donors will need to reconcile the two approaches outlined in this section to form a unified strategy that best leverages collective international donor support.

In broad strokes, the Haitian government and donors agree on *what* needs to be done: recruit, educate, and train teachers; develop quality standards; resolve the long-standing debate about the place of French and Haitian Creole in the curriculum; create a system for enforcing quality standards; and greatly expand the provision of education (especially in rural areas) to ultimately allow all children to obtain a formal basic education. Disagreement arises over *who* should do these things, *when* specific reforms should occur, in what order, and *how* they should be implemented.[40]

The central debate among international donors turns on differences over the best means of achieving sustainable reform. One group (particularly the IDB, supported by the Louisiana school superintendent Paul Vallas and Haitian first lady Elisabeth Préval) advocates the creation of an administrative structure that would operate independently of the MENFP. After a period of five years, this education recovery authority would disband and the MENFP would then assume responsibility for reforms that the donor-led recovery authority had achieved. In this view, leaving responsibility for all reforms with

---

[40] Telephone conversation with representative of donor organization 1, May 2010.

the current MENFP will produce few, if any results. However, if the MENFP does not support the externally led reforms, then it may not take the necessary steps to ensure their long-term success.

Other donors (particularly the World Bank) argue that, "without capacity, there is no development."[41] In other words, to the greatest degree possible, the MENFP should lead the effort to set out education policies. The World Bank advocates implementing a sustainable set of reforms that are more authentically Haitian-led. It relies on the Haitian government sustaining political will and direction—an assumption that Haiti's decades of government churn belies.

Each of these approaches acknowledges that the Haitian government has to own education reforms and its authority to select which elements are most in its interest. Donors are working with one another to potentially merge the two approaches. However, the two views epitomize a long-standing debate: whether donors should direct reforms themselves or whether they should work at the behest of the Haitian government.

IDB: Develop an Externally Run School Recovery Authority. In February 2010, the IDB circulated a draft proposal for the reconstruction and reorganization of Haiti's school system.[42] Costed out at approximately $2 billion to operate the entire education system for five years, the IDB plan proposes a short-term strategy for 2010–2011 to return teachers and children to school and a 2010–2015 strategy—the main element of which is a donor-led recovery authority with both policymaking and implementation functions.[43] To date, the IDB has committed $250 million toward this $2 billion plan, of which $19 million

---

[41] This phrase comes from the title of a UNESCO-sponsored report about improving the capacity of organizations and not just individuals (De Grauwe, 2009).

[42] IDB (2010).

[43] Annualized over five years, $2 billion barely exceeds pre-earthquake spending on education, including public and private, in Haiti. Wolff (2008) estimates (using MENFP, 2007, sources) that the government spent $82.9 million on education in 2006 and annual spending on private education was $276 million. Updated into 2010 dollars, this amounts to approximately $387 million per year.

was committed prior to the earthquake.[44] The balance of the $2 billion would be required from other donors and from the Haitian government. The IDB estimate of $2 billion is preliminary, and it likely underestimates the true costs of the proposed reforms.

The core of the IDB proposal is the longer-term 2010–2015 strategy to create an independently run education recovery authority to develop and operate the following: (1) a federated model of schooling with public funding for private, public, and charter-like schools; (2) a national curriculum that incorporates French, English, and Haitian Creole; (3) a system for recruiting and training teachers and administrators modeled on U.S. programs, such as Teach for America or New Leaders for New Schools; (4) school facilities that are designed to withstand natural disasters; (5) a financial model and accounting system for a tuition-free education; and (6) a system of social services for delivery at schools.[45] After five years, the recovery authority would disband and the MENFP would assume all of these functions. The division of authority between the MENFP and the recovery authority during 2010–2015 is not outlined; perhaps MSNFP officials would staff part of the recovery authority. But it is clear from the IDB proposal that it would run parallel to the MENFP (with some phasing in of MENFP oversight over time) and that a third party would administer the funds—presumably a set of international donors to an education trust fund.

In concert with the IDB, Paul Vallas, the current superintendent of the Recovery School District in Louisiana and former superintendent of schools in Philadelphia and Chicago, put forward an April 2010 draft proposal for a recovery authority that resembles Louisiana's Recovery School District. Similar to the February IDB draft, the Vallas proposal leaves unanswered the questions whether the MENFP would establish the policy priorities of the authority and how the MENFP's ability to exercise its functions would be enhanced through working with the recovery authority.

---

[44] Telephone conversation with representative of a multilateral organization, May 2010.

[45] Vallas (2010).

World Bank: Ministry Establishes Policies and Donors Execute Them. The World Bank's top priority for education is to develop one coordinated donor strategy and avoid duplicative or contradictory donor engagement with the government of Haiti.[46] To this end, the World Bank has not proposed its own strategy. Instead, it advocates a process of multilateral collaboration with the MENFP to craft a rebuilding strategy; it has opposed the IDB's proposed external education authority.[47] The World Bank advocates that the primary MENFP role should be to formulate education policy, which donors should then implement.

In the World Bank's view, Haiti's 2010 PDNA establishes the main elements of what should be done to resuscitate and improve the educational system. To enact the PDNA elements, the MENFP has approached donors with a list of 13 specialty areas in which it has requested consultants to work as part of its staff, assuming a role much like the head of a division within the MENFP. These specialty areas are testing and assessment, early-childhood education, legal counsel, budget planning, strategic planning, public-private partnerships, school facilities, accreditation/regulation, building operations and maintenance, national curriculum, coordination of aid, education policy, and teacher training.[48]

According to the World Bank, the hired specialists could aid the MENFP in developing policies, and then the execution of those policies could be outsourced to a set of external donors. Specifically, each donor from a collective task force could adopt one of the 13 policy areas. For example, an attenuated version of a recovery authority that the IDB proposes (see previous section) could oversee the construction of schools. France could lead teacher training; the World Bank, public-private partnerships; and on down the list of the 13 policy areas. A donor committee would control an education trust fund that would finance the implementation of education policies. The first donor into

---

[46] Telephone conversation with representative of donor organization 1, May 2010.

[47] Telephone conversation with representative of donor organization 2, April 2010; telephone conversation with representative of donor organization 1, May 2010.

[48] MENFP (2010b).

the fund could be the Catalytic Fund (with $22 million), following by CIDA, the EU, Spain, the Caribbean Development Bank, and so on.[49]

Pros and Cons of the Two Proposals. The key distinction between the World Bank model and the IDB's proposed recovery authority is that, in the World Bank's version, the MENFP would retain all policymaking functions. In that sense, the World Bank's advocated model is more in line with the pre-earthquake model of donor activity, in which donors often specialized in particular areas of service delivery on behalf of, or in place of, the government. The IDB proposal is grander in scope and proposes an organizational structure that does not entirely align with the set of priority areas that the MENFP has thus far identified.

There are, of course, trade-offs between the World Bank and IDB proposals. An externally led education recovery authority, such as the IDB proposes, might instill greater donor confidence and thus attract more funding. However, an approach that leaves decisionmaking with the MENFP might better achieve buy-in from the Haitian government and result in a plan that is more responsive to Haiti's situation.

Recommendations

The ultimate and unfortunately very long-term goal of education reform should be to provide a free, universal education of sufficient quality to equip Haiti's children with the skills and knowledge that translate into improved material circumstances and overall well-being. In the short run (one to two years), the Haitian government and donors' first order of business is the quickest possible resumption of schooling and the provision of temporary school facilities. The recommendations we set out in this section focus on medium-term means (three to five years) to progress toward the goal of quality education. In the long run (five to 20 years), a stable educational system that is truly universal will require a much larger government role in education, including the direct pro-

[49] Prior to the earthquake, both Canada and Spain had signed letters of intent to contribute to the Catalytic Fund, but neither country has yet committed funds specifically to education out of their overall commitments made at the March 31, 2010, donor conference (telephone conversation with representative of a multilateral organization, May 2010).

vision of free public-sector schooling. The exact model for a federated system of public and private schooling is impossible to determine at this early stage, but the strengthening of the MENFP's role in the medium term would pave the way for expanded direct public provision of education in the future.

Considering the dire condition of education in Haiti at all levels—elementary, secondary, and postsecondary—the following recommendations focus on rebuilding the elementary level as the top priority. This aligns with the country's own EFA commitment to provide all children with a basic formal education.

Although short-term measures are necessary to prevent multiyear interruption of educational services to children in the aftermath of the earthquake, they should be understood as suboptimal solutions in service of the longer-term systemic reconfiguration of education in Haiti. Ultimately, a cadre of trained professionals is required to operate an education system of sufficient quality to improve social and economic conditions in Haiti.

Strengthen Government Oversight

Donors often invoke the need to "build capacity" in Haiti's state institutions, but it is rarely achieved. Implementation of capacity-building activities is expensive, slow, and often prone to failure—whether through unpredicted changes in leadership, attrition from the organization of those individuals who received training, or a failure by outside trainers to appreciate the context and incentive systems in which local staff work.[50] But it is a necessary, albeit high-risk, investment. No matter what shape the education recovery plan takes, improved quality of and access to education will require a substantial increase in the number and skill set of MENFP employees. *A medium-term recovery plan should not establish an externally led governance structure parallel to the MENFP; instead, it should work with the MENFP to expand its size and invest heavily in staff capacity and skills to regulate schools and set out education reform policy.*

---

[50] De Grauwe (2009).

Specifically, a redevelopment plan should be organized around explicit *steps to develop a cadre of mid- and lower-level managers within the MENFP to set standards for schools and to regulate accredited schools.* Such steps might include payment for MENFP salaries to increase the size of the MENFP and the placement of outside specialists in roles within the MENFP that evolve from leads to coaches over a period of five to ten years. The Haitian diaspora could provide a potential source of skilled employees to staff the MENFP. The MENFP's capacities to regulate and steadily fund the provision of education are the two most important aspects of sustainability of reform. To achieve improved quality of schooling through increased investments in teachers and in oversight of schools, the MENFP needs to have the capacity to accredit schools in the first place, periodically inspect schools to assess their continued compliance, and oversee the transfer of funds to eligible schools for teacher wage subsidies (discussed under "Improve Quality"). It also requires that the MENFP have the capacity to enforce a fair system of teacher training (whether it is privately or publicly run) and testing of teachers.

To develop the MENFP's ability to regulate and finance the primary-education system over the next three to five years, an education recovery plan should include substantial funding for investment in maintaining a staff and in developing the technical skills of those who will remain in the MENFP after donors leave. Whether consultants to the MENFP or externally led entities oversee the initial development of educational delivery systems, the MENFP will ultimately need to oversee these functions. Without trained staff, even the best investments in teacher training, school accreditation, school-choice systems, national curriculum, and social services are at risk of failure over the long run.

Expand Access

Substantially improving the quality of education will require building a qualified teacher corps, which will take many years. In the meantime, stopgap interventions to increase the availability of educational opportunities should run concurrently to teacher training and phase out as the supply of teachers grows.

Interventions, such as contract teachers and the expansion of radio programming, can help to fill immediate needs for delivery of education. Unlike the longer-term development of a teacher corps described under "Improve Quality," schools could immediately hire teachers on annual renewable contracts. Low-paid contract teachers have been shown to positively affect student performance in Kenya, most so when local school committees were permitted to monitor the teachers.[51] Contract teachers would be equivalent to entry-level private-sector teachers in Haiti. As such, they do not necessarily hold promise to improve the quality of education but would be a measure to open classrooms in the near term. An approach much along these lines is already contemplated in the April 2010 MENFP proposal for resuming school activities, but it will need to expand into the next one to two years. Unlike the teacher payment system described under "Improve Quality," short-term contract teachers would not have to meet standards of demonstrated proficiency on teacher tests and thus should not be eligible for the same set of proposed wage subsidies.

Those who helped design the content and the delivery system for the math and Creole radio programming in the 1990s—USAID (which funded the programming), the Haitian Foundation for Private Education, and contractors, such as the Education Development Center—could help craft the expansion of radio programming as a temporary measure to provide children with a modicum of continued content instruction. Radio programming has the advantage of being low cost while widely disseminating content of known quality. It can reach children in both rural and urban settings, and it can improve the quality of instruction in situations in which teachers are simply absent or lack mastery of the material.

To improve children's well-being and to increase their attendance, schools should also provide meals and basic health services to students. Building on the World Food Programme's ongoing school feeding program, donors should expand their assistance to the government of Haiti to provide food and health services to children at all school sites. Both

---

[51] Duflo, Kremer, and Dupas (2010). These researchers obtained similar results in India.

services have been shown in randomized controlled trials to have statistically significant and large positive effects on student attendance.[52]

Improve Quality

Improving teacher quality in the private and public sectors should be the top priority of a mid- and longer-term education improvement plan, regardless of who designs or administers it. One of the principal barriers to both expanding the provision of education (whether in the public or private sector) and to increasing the quality of schooling is the lack of sufficiently qualified people to meet the demand for teachers. Without teachers who are fully literate and know the material they are teaching, redesigned curricula or textbooks would have minimal impact on improving children's educational outcomes. Improving teacher quality, which will take many years, should phase in immediately, with content training provided to a first teacher cohort starting in 2011–2012.

To help close the quality gap between private and public schools and to increase access to schools, the MENFP should subsidize private-sector teacher wages to be on par with public-sector salaries. However, teacher wage subsidies should be conditioned on compliance with a series of incentives for schools to become accredited and for teachers to demonstrate academic proficiency. Better salaries are essential to sustaining any improvements in teacher quality over time. To achieve this, the wage increment should be available only to teachers working in accredited schools that charge capped (minimal) fees to families and enroll a minimum number of students. The wage supplement creates an incentive for private schools to enter into and annually maintain quality standards required for accreditation (such as the teaching of core subjects, building safety and quality-of-care minimums, and standardized recordkeeping regarding teachers and students). Schools must then pay out the publicly funded wage increase only to those teachers in accredited schools who received training, demonstrated proficiency on tests of the content they are to teach, and meet minimum attendance require-

---

52 See research experiments in Kenya and India (J-PAL, undated).

ments.[53] The private/public teacher salary schedule could be phased in with graduating cohorts of trained teachers.

Given the lack of an educated middle class in Haiti from which to draw for teachers, several proposals have been made to attract nonresidents to form a teacher corps, such as a Teach for Haiti, modeled on Teach for America. Such a program could be designed to appeal to both young college graduates and the Haitian diaspora. A Teach for Haiti–type program might attract a *limited* number of well-educated, qualified teachers (Teach for America accepted a 2008 cohort of approximately 3,600 new teachers for the entire United States). However, Haiti needs approximately 60,000 teachers to lead classrooms, which means that the vast majority of teachers will have to come from within the country. Investing in Haitian teachers will not only improve schooling, but it will also establish a large source of employment in the country. Considering the poor educational attainment of the teachers, *programs to prepare teachers should focus primarily on the content teachers are to convey to students and secondarily on pedagogical instruction.*[54]

To provide a stable source of funds for teacher improvement, private-sector teachers' wages should be included in donors' midterm education aid packages. An internationally funded commitment to pay a portion of private- (and possibly public-) sector teachers' wages over a number of years would help to restore confidence in and increase the attractiveness of the teaching profession. It could also provide donors influence in setting the conditions teachers must satisfy, as well as in establishing an escalating schedule of wages for desired teacher and school characteristics and practices. Further, a wage schedule could structure rewards for remaining in the profession and for the continued attainment of education and training. As discussed earlier, the MENFP should considerably increase its oversight to enforce these requirements as a condition for cash transfers to schools for teacher wages.

---

[53] As supported by experimentally designed research of Indian teachers in Duflo, Hanna, and Ryan (2008).

[54] Haiti's existing national education plan and its system of student testing could serve as the provisional standards for teacher training, with subsequent revision of a national curriculum led by the MENFP in future years.

In international research, teacher quality is considered the most important of the school characteristics influencing student achievement.[55] As such, it is perhaps the single most important element of schooling in which Haiti could invest.

---

[55] For a discussion, see Eide, Goldhaber, and Brewer (2004).

CHAPTER NINE

Health

The Challenges

Long-Standing Challenges

Health services in Haiti were and continue to be delivered through four channels: public institutions, including state-run health centers and referral hospitals; private, nonprofit organizations; mixed public and nonprofit institutions owned by the state but operated by NGOs, whose staff work alongside public employees; and private, for-profit medical offices in Port-au-Prince and other large cities. The Ministère de la Santé Publique et de la Population (MSPP, or Ministry of Public Health and Population) is responsible for the public health system, including the delivery of health services, policymaking and implementation, and management of the government's health budget.

Prior to the earthquake, the Haitian health sector was already in poor condition. Although the Haitian constitution calls for universal access to health care, approximately 40 percent of the population lacked access to care, particularly in rural areas of the country.[1] Lack of access has two dimensions: lack of physical access, as 13 percent of the population lives more than 15 kilometers away from the nearest health center, and lack of financial access, as cost-recovery policies in place in most institutions require fees for services that are unaffordable to a large proportion of the population.

In addition, hospital, clinic, laboratory, and medical teaching facilities commonly experienced electric-power blackouts and short-

[1] PAHO (2007, p. 1).

ages of water.[2] Many buildings were in poor condition; most facilities were outdated; and much of the medical equipment was old or broken.

The MSPP does not have systems in place to track health status and monitor quality of care. For example, only an estimated one in 20 deaths results in a death certificate that documents cause of death. Biannual childhood immunization campaigns do not include documentation of vaccines given—either for the MSPP or for immunized individuals.[3] This lack of basic public health information leads to a host of quality issues within the health system. For example, immunization coverage is suspected to be low, and duplicate immunizations not uncommon. In addition, there is little reliable data from which to determine priority health policies and programs.

The MSPP has little human capital or administrative capacity to carry out its functions. A lack of not only doctors and nurses but also administrative professionals has been a major challenge. While current numbers for physician density in Haiti are not generally available, in 2001, Haiti had only three physicians for every 10,000 inhabitants;[4] most were concentrated in the capital. This compares poorly with rates in the Dominican Republic (19), for example, and is the lowest rate in Latin America and the Caribbean.[5] Many health professionals have been lost to the diaspora over the years. For those who have stayed, there are few incentives to work in rural or underserved areas of the country or exclusively in public institutions. An agreement with Cuba has allowed for the staffing of some rural clinics with Cuban healthcare professionals. However, like other aspects of the health system, this program is not properly managed for quality. The MSPP also lacks adequate technical and administrative staff for policy, planning, and regulatory functions—particularly at the mid level, as well as outside of the central offices in Port-au-Prince.

---

2 PAHO (2010a, p. 3).

3 PAHO (2010a, p. 2).

4 PAHO (2003, p. 6).

5 WHO (undated).

Although the MSPP has formal responsibility for regulating and monitoring Haiti's health-care system, it has never truly performed this role. There are no consistent accreditation procedures for health-care facilities or training institutions, and no official certification exams for medical professionals to practice in the country. When the MSPP has set policies or regulations, it has had no means to enforce them. The lack of reliable health outcome data in Haiti has made monitoring the quality of health services nearly impossible. Although there have been calls to improve quality-control systems for pharmaceuticals and ensure standardization of medicines, little to no progress had been made on this front.

The MSPP has played only a minor role in financing health care. Prior to the earthquake, the health sector was receiving the largest amount of foreign aid of all service sectors in Haiti. Between 2003 and 2007, 18 to 30 percent of bilateral commitments for aid to Haiti were designated for health and population programs.[6] Of all spending on health services, at least 50 percent was provided by donors. The government only covered 15 percent of health-care spending from its budget; individuals covered 35 percent of costs out of their own pockets.[7] About 90 percent of the government's health budget was used to cover salaries for MSPP employees, so almost all operating expenses, capital outlays, and health plans and programs were funded by external, often uncoordinated, actors.

Such extensive donor involvement has created a logistical challenge for the government that it has been unable to overcome: the need to coordinate, regulate, and oversee donor and implementer plans and activities. Donors, in general, have been unwilling to provide budget support to the MSPP and have often operated independently—leading to both duplication and gaps in service delivery. In many senses, health-care coverage and quality have been dictated by donors and their implementers with little to no government oversight of their operations or influence on their programming and with little coordination among donors.

---

6 OECD (2009, p. 148).

7 PAHO (2003, p. 11).

The lack of a coherent, structured health system in Haiti has led to poor health outcomes. Average life expectancy was estimated to be 60 years in 2007, one of eight out of 38 countries in Latin America and the Caribbean with a life expectancy at birth of less than 70 years.[8] The most-prevalent and most-severe health problems affecting the Haitian population include the following:

- *Low immunization rates:* The coverage rates for children under one year of age for three common immunizations—measles, diphtheria-pertussis-tetanus (DPT), and polio—are 54 percent, 68 percent, and 66 percent, respectively.[9] This is well below typical rates of more than 90 percent for other countries in the region.[10]
- *Prevalence of vector-borne diseases:* Malaria, dengue, and other vectorborne diseases have very high prevalence rates relative to other countries in the region.[11]
- *Human immunodeficiency virus (HIV)/acquired immunodeficiency syndrome (AIDS):* The Haitian prevalence of HIV/AIDS is 2.2 percent in the adult population, higher than any country outside of sub-Saharan Africa. The HIV/tuberculosis (TB) co-infection rate was near 30 percent prior to the earthquake.[12]
- *High infant mortality:* The under-five mortality rate is 86 deaths per 1,000 live births, up from 76 per 1,000 live births in 2007. This is the highest in the region by a large margin.[13] Acute respiratory infections and diarrheal diseases were among the leading causes of death in children under five.[14]

---

8 WHO (undated).

9 PAHO (2010a, p. 3).

10 WHO (undated).

11 PAHO (2010a, p. 3).

12 PAHO (2010a, p. 3).

13 WHO (undated).

14 PAHO (2010a, p. 3).

Consequences of the Earthquake

Health Needs. Most of the people displaced by the earthquake now live in crowded tent camps that are prone to the spread of vectorborne and communicable diseases. The earthquake injured an estimated 300,000 people, in addition to traumatizing a large part of Haiti's population.[15] As a consequence, there is a great need to monitor and prevent vectorborne and contagious diseases within the camps, treat mental illnesses stemming from the earthquake, ensure that interrupted treatment regimes are resumed, provide prosthetics for people who have lost limbs, and provide occupational and rehabilitative medicine.

Infrastructure. The MSPP offices have been destroyed and nearby medical and nursing schools severely damaged. The MSPP is currently working out of tents and makeshift locations. It is unclear when a more permanent structure will become available. Many hospitals and clinics have also been damaged or destroyed. Estimated losses, public and private, total almost $3 billion; 73 out of 373 hospitals, health clinics, training institutes, and other facilities have experienced severe damage or complete destruction.[16]

Information Management and Records. Paper records, files, and accounting and operations information that were stored in destroyed MSPP buildings are now lost. This is also the case for the hospitals and other facilities that were destroyed or damaged.[17] Despite poor record management prior to the earthquake, the destruction of what did exist in terms of patient, administrative, and operational records severely reduces the ability of MSPP to work toward quality and continuity of care as well as to implement previous plans and objectives for health-sector operations and improvements.

Human Capital. Human-capital losses were significant; MSPP alone lost 200 staff when its building in Port-au-Prince collapsed.[18]

---

[15] Private Sector Economic Forum (2010, p. 21).

[16] PAHO (undated).

[17] Republic of Haiti (2010b, p. 61).

[18] PAHO (2010b, p. 4).

Many health workers were killed or seriously injured. The influx of humanitarian assistance immediately following the earthquake has ameliorated the lack of human resources for the short term, but this supply will dissipate and Haiti's shortage of health-care professionals will be more acute than ever. Compounding the problem is the destruction of medical training centers.

Health-care providers in rural areas have been stretched even further by the influx of people who have left quake-affected cities. The health-care system's lack of capacity to respond adequately means that many people may return to the cities to seek care.

The already limited management capacity within the MSPP has been taxed by the influx of donors after the earthquake. The need for additional coordination and monitoring of donor activities has overwhelmed the MSPP; many donors are acting independently. Donor coordination has also "crowded out" other essential activities from the MSPP's agenda, including detailed planning for the medium to long term.

Adverse Long-Term Effects of Humanitarian Aid. Policies for and donor involvement in the disaster-relief phase are likely producing adverse, unintended consequences that will affect the ability of the health sector to develop over the long run. First and foremost, there has been a large influx in the number of well-trained, donor-funded health professionals who are providing relatively high-quality health care for free to displaced persons in the tent camps. In addition, the government called for free care to be offered to those in need for three months after the earthquake and has recently extended this policy for an additional three months. Free health services have been necessary to respond to the crisis, but the proliferation of free health care has resulted in several hospitals that rely on fees to operate shutting down. Whether these institutions will be able to reopen once the disaster-relief phase passes remains a question. This policy also has shifted expectations among the Haitian population toward access to free care. This has the potential to undermine MSPP efforts in the medium and longer terms to build a fiscally sustainable health system.

Appraisal of Plans and Initiatives for Addressing the Challenges

Plans and Initiatives Before the Earthquake

In an effort to improve health service delivery, the Haitian government established a strategy in the late 1990s centered on a Basic Health Services Package (BHSP)—a bundle of essential services that was to be made available to all Haitians. The BHSP was to be delivered through the establishment of community health units (unités communales de santé, or UCSs), established in an attempt to restructure the health system in line with national plans for decentralization of government. The UCSs were not organized along existing political or geographical boundaries, raising concerns about coordination of health services with other social services organized at the department, commune, or communal-section level.

All health-sector plans since the 1990s have focused on expanding the BHSP through the decentralized UCS system, as well as strengthening regulation of the health sector. Successive plans have continued to focus on these same objectives, since little progress in implementing reforms has been achieved over the years.

Strategic Plan for Health Sector Reform. The primary plan in place for health prior to the earthquake was the five-year *Strategic Plan for Health Sector Reform.*[19] This was the most recent of the MSPP's five-year plans but had changed very little from previous iterations. The previous plan had been published in 2004 and covered the period of 2003–2008. Both the 2003–2008 and the 2005–2010 plans were comprehensive in covering needs for reform but set no priorities among these needs, nor did they specify an implementation timeline, responsible parties, resources available, or how progress would be monitored. In addition, proposed activities were not necessarily sufficient for achieving overall objectives. For example, plans for developing human resources to ensure that the entire population receives high-quality health services focused entirely on the Haitian public health–sector

---

[19] MSPP (2004).

workforce. This focus is insufficient given Haiti's current reliance on NGOs and Cuban health professionals to deliver care.

Each of the plans laid out the same eight primary objectives and virtually the same actions to be taken, as well as expected results, by the end of the planning time horizon. These objectives included (1) decentralizing the health system, (2) improving access to health-care services, (3) improving the public hospital network, (4) enhancing health-sector regulation, (5) modernizing health information systems, (6) developing human resources for health, (7) guaranteeing access to essential drugs, and (8) developing financial resources to support the health sector. The MSPP published the plans, but UNICEF, the Pan American Health Organization (PAHO)/World Health Organization (WHO), and the United Nations Population Fund helped develop them by providing technical assistance.

GPRSP. The Haitian government's GPRSP also touches on the health sector. Although the objectives and strategies put forth in this paper were similar to, and certainly not in conflict with, the MSPP's plans, a stronger emphasis was placed on developing a national health policy and its component parts, updating laws necessary for regulation based on policy, and establishing procedures for inspecting and assessing health activities. The paper included eight somewhat different objectives for the health sector, including (1) progress toward meeting Haiti's MDGs, (2) revitalizing and expanding the hospital network, (3) strengthening UCSs, (4) improving support for priority illnesses, (5) developing policy on access to essential drugs, (6) developing policies to strengthen health-sector governance, (7) developing policies for human-resource development, and (8) establishing hospital waste-management policy. The paper included "strategic lines of action" for each of these objectives, but, like the MSPP's five-year plans, included no discussion of implementation, such as setting priorities or a sequence for actions, timelines, responsible parties, financial resources, or means for monitoring progress.

ICF. Although not a reform plan, the ICF put in place after the 2004 crisis was used by the Haitian government as a mechanism for donor coordination and planning. The framework called for the establishment of "sector tables" to address the fragmented, parallel, and often duplicative nature of donor involvement in Haiti. The health-sector table, comprised of MSPP officials and bilateral and multilateral donors, developed a set of sector priorities: (1) restart the operation of principal hospitals, (2) extend the reach of the BHSP, (3) strengthen the management and coordination capacity of the MSPP, (4) improve the population's access to health care, and (5) restart priority programs for the purchase and distribution of essential drugs.[20] The health-sector table was helpful in prioritizing needs and setting the agenda for donor involvement. However, the sector tables did not include private organizations (important players in Haiti's health sector); arrangements were nonbinding; and there was no implementation plan or means for monitoring progress.

All of the plans produced prior to the earthquake addressed key needs of Haiti's health sector; the MSPP's plans in particular are quite comprehensive. However, the plans did not set priorities, specify activities for achieving objectives, or propose an appropriate sequencing of such activities. Given the state of Haiti's health system, the list of planned improvements is long—and, given the constrained human and financial resources, the MSPP needs to focus on feasible first steps based on priorities and plan for implementation over time.

Revised Plans

PDNA. The 2010 PDNA is not a plan but provides useful planning guidance in that it focuses not only on what is needed to rebuild in the short term but also what the goals of reconstruction should be over the next ten years. Unlike past plans, it sets priorities for health. It calls for focusing on decentralization, strengthening the MSPP to set policies for and regulate the health system, and enhancing human-resource capacity. It also suggests four strategic aims for the health sector over the long term: (1) refining the service package at each level of care and reorganizing the delivery system, including intersectoral community strategies (e.g., nutrition, sanitation); (2) improving governance within the health sector and introducing a performance-based funding system; (3) channeling significant investment into human

---

[20] Republic of Haiti (2004).

resources; and (4) improving the way in which material inputs and essential drugs are managed and improving patient transport and communication resources. The PDNA does not outline ways to go about defining achievable goals or set forth a plan or timeline for developing a more concrete, actionable agenda.

Action Plan for the National Recovery and Development of Haiti. The government's postearthquake action plan focuses on an 18-month time frame but is tied to the ten-year vision laid out in the PDNA. The health component is focused on rebuilding infrastructure, investing in human resources, and strengthening the management of inputs and essential medicines. Budgetary needs are put forward but with little detail on how funds would be used. The document does, however, explicitly address the need for donors to work under the direction of the MSPP in order to bolster the MSPP's legitimacy and authority for the future.

Plan Intérimaire du Secteur Santé. The interim plan for the health sector was developed by the MSPP, with donor-provided technical assistance, as an elaboration of the action plan's provisions for the health sector. The document outlines five major goals: (1) service delivery in quake-affected areas, (2) ensuring service provision in camps, (3) ensuring continuity of service while adjusting to emerging and longer-term needs, (4) maintaining and strengthening MSPP at all levels, and (5) establishing the basis for long-term improvements in health care. With a major focus on short- and medium-term priorities, the document advocates improving primary care, particularly by expanding the basic package of services offered through mobile clinics at the UCS level to include mental health, rehabilitation, and nutrition—areas in which needs have increased because of the earthquake. Additionally, it establishes human resources as a high priority and calls for a specific action plan to be developed to increase human capacity within the MSPP. Like the five-year *Strategic Plan for Health Sector Reform*, however, it focuses on training Haitians without consideration of other critical resources, such as NGO staff, Cuban health professionals, and health professionals from the Haitian diaspora.

Although the plan is well thought out and comprehensive in general areas of need, it has the same deficiencies as pre-earthquake plans: no prioritization or specificity. The document covers everything from a revised basic package of health services to improving the state of research and medical education, to improving the provision of and access to drugs, to developing a unified information system for health records. Each objective is accompanied by several action items, but objectives are not prioritized, and most action items are not specific. The MSPP, however, is currently working with major health donors on a more detailed document that will specify who will take responsibility for each component of the plan.[21]

Private Sector Economic Forum *Vision and Roadmap for Haiti*. The Private Sector Economic Forum's proposal for Haiti's redevelopment in the short, medium, and long terms includes a short section devoted to the health sector. The timeline for this document stretches out five years but has ramifications for long-term development. This document, unlike others discussed here, helpfully identifies clear indicators of progress toward the goals it has specified and timelines to achieve these goals. For example, in the case of providing mental-health services to people affected by trauma, the road map defines an indicator of success as the number of people who received psychosocial counseling and support or the number of camps covered. In addition, the group recognizes practical limitations, such as the lack of trained professionals, and suggests possible alternatives.[22]

The road map is biased toward issues with which the private sector can help (e.g., surveillance systems, supply-chain management, health insurance and other financing schemes). It is a useful document with some very good ideas. It addresses pragmatic, operational, and very real issues with which the MSPP and donors will have to deal, as funds and talent for instituting reforms are limited.

---

[21] Telephone discussion with donor-agency representative, May 2010.

[22] Private Sector Economic Forum (2010, p. 21).

Recommendations

The MSPP's progress in implementing its five-year plans, including provision of the BHSP through the UCS structure, may well have been undermined by the plans' lack of prioritization and specificity. Of all the plans on the table prior to the earthquake, none contained the detail necessary for successful implementation. Plans proposed post-earthquake—specifically the MSPP's *Plan Intérimaire du Secteur Santé* and the Private Sector Economic Forum's *Vision and Roadmap for Haiti*—are quite similar. Both include new ideas and additions to the old plans, but neither offers sufficient prioritization or specific actions toward implementation. A truly useful plan to improve Haiti's health sector must incorporate an honest assessment of what *has* to be done, what *can* be done, and then *how* these objectives can be accomplished in a way that builds the capacity of the MSPP.

In this section, we propose strategic priorities and key implementation measures for the next three to five years, aimed at moving toward a health system in Haiti that is both feasible and sustainable. These proposals draw on components of existing plans but elaborate those components and narrow the focus. The recommendations include some new approaches for achieving agreed-upon objectives and adhere to the principles of being simple and practical; strengthening the capacity of the MSPP and Haiti's health sector in general; achieving visible results; and ensuring that results are attributed to the Haitian government—and the MSPP in particular.

Focus on Strengthening Policymaking, Planning, Regulation, and Oversight

The MSPP has not worked to develop a true public health system in Haiti. It has tended to accept, without challenge, well-intentioned, but often duplicative, low-priority, or one-off donor initiatives rather than to set a health policy agenda and then ask donors to conform to this agenda. *The MSPP should seek technical assistance from donors to develop and implement an actionable national health strategy (i.e., with specified priorities, actions, and timeline), along with related policies, programs, and regulatory and oversight mechanisms.* Examples include setting the requirements for any health service–delivery contracts (e.g., defining the basic package of health services that must be provided, and setting the cost and payment structure for services); establishing systems and rules for the procurement and distribution of medical supplies, equipment, and pharmaceuticals; designing and implementing national public health surveillance and information systems; and developing related monitoring and enforcement systems. The MSPP's focus on such activities to strengthen the health system, including building capacity to carry out these activities over time, would enhance the donor community's trust in the MSPP and thus increase donors' willingness to directly support the MSPP.

Establish Performance-Based Contracting Mechanism for Provision of Services

The MSPP's planning documents for health-sector reform all call for universal access to care and a distributed network of primary (health centers), secondary (community referral hospitals), and tertiary (department referral hospitals) facilities operated by the MSPP. Many of these institutions are currently run by NGOs, while others remain empty, understaffed, or inconsistently staffed. In addition, donors and NGOs are establishing new operations to fill gaps and are paying the bulk of the operating costs and capital expenses for Haiti's network of health services.

The MSPP needs to gain control over the delivery of health services in Haiti to ensure achievement of its goal of universal access to a consistent set of services. Given the lack of capacity and funding within the MSPP today and in the foreseeable future, *consideration should be given to shifting the operation of* all *health centers and hospitals to NGOs and other private institutions, allowing the MSPP to concentrate on setting policy and planning for, overseeing, monitoring, and evaluating the operation of Haiti's public health service–delivery network.*

The MSPP, with donor technical and funding assistance, could establish its own performance-based contracting mechanism for the provision of health services throughout the country. All health services (first-tier health centers, as well as referral hospitals) within each UCS, or some other appropriate geographical division, could be contracted as a bundle to ensure continuity of care. To build capacity, department-, UCS-, or other community-level MSPP employees could be fully involved in contracting and oversight activities. The World Bank could be a partner for the MSPP to develop and implement such a program, given its experience with these programs elsewhere; the minister has already expressed interest in this idea.

Having the MSPP plan for and contract out the delivery of health-care services by UCS (or some other geographic boundary) could ensure equitable access to and provision of care, in line with the MSPP's current goals; ensure improvements in priority health conditions by setting and holding contractors accountable to measurable goals; help to standardize and stabilize salaries for public-sector health workers; ensure continuity of care through referrals and counterreferrals within the same service-delivery management structure; eliminate inefficient duplication of health services; and allow the MSPP to concentrate on developing the policies, planning, and oversight mechanisms essential for an effective health-care system. The MSPP could build specific requirements into its service-delivery contracts (e.g., service branding and signage rules) to ensure that health services maintain a government "face" and that the government receives credit for its provision of health services. The MSPP could also consider contracting out shared services (e.g., medical waste disposal, central and decentralized laboratories) for Haiti's public health service–delivery network. Such efforts could help control health-care costs, ensure quality of support services and materials, and support local Haitian businesses.

Ultimately, this reform will require sufficient MSPP funds for letting service contracts and for supporting MSPP staff and operations at the central (policy and planning) and decentralized (oversight and implementation) levels. Although Haitian government expenditures on the health sector ought to be significantly increased over time, substantial increases in funding from the Haitian government are unlikely over the next three to five years. Thus, donors will need to continue to pay for the bulk of Haiti's health-care costs, including the technical and administrative infrastructure required to build a sustainable health system. Under a performance contracting approach, however, the MSPP, supported by donor technical assistance and a commitment to coordination, would take control over where and how health care is provided in Haiti. This would be an improvement over the current state of affairs, in which the MSPP is not fully aware or in control of where and how health care is provided across the country.

Donors initially would need to directly fund services for their "assigned" areas of the country, but, over time, as the MSPP's capacity expands, donors should channel their funding through the MSPP. Those donors engaged in building the technical capacity of MSPP employees at the central, department, and commune levels initially would need to work jointly with MSPP staff to develop and implement MSPP plans, policies, and programs. Such arrangements should include cash transfers to the MSPP to allow for appropriate staff hires, office space, and the purchase of required equipment.

Reorganize Decentralized Health-Care Operations

Decentralization has been a key component of health-sector planning for many years. It is a primary strategy for ensuring universal access to a basic package of health services. However, the plan to develop and implement UCSs across the country as a means for decentralization has never been fully realized. Lack of ministerial management capability and financing have been major contributors to the failure of UCS implementation, but an added complication is that the UCSs do not conform to the political and community lines around which other government services are organized in Haiti. *As a first step in a renewed effort toward decentralization in the health sector, the MSPP should reorganize its decentralized operations based on department and commune lines.* This will permit improved integration with other government service delivery and a more natural "bundling" of health services (i.e., referral and counterreferral systems among health centers, community hospitals, and department hospitals) to contract out to service-delivery providers. Such "bundled" performance-based contracts can be developed and monitored by decentralized MSPP staff at the department or commune level and would provide an opportunity for them to work closely with providers in the area on developing and monitoring regional health goals, among other initiatives.

Build Human-Resource Capacity

The MSPP's five-year strategic plans developed before the earthquake and the more recent health-sector interim plan address the need for developing human-resource capacity within Haiti's health sector. They focus on improving the quality of the current Haitian health-care professional workforce. They also stress bolstering the educational institutions that train Haiti's future health-care professionals. In continued planning efforts for developing Haiti's health-care professional workforce, use of NGO staff, Cuban health-care professionals, and health professionals in the Haitian diaspora should be considered, as well as the development of paraprofessionals, such as midwives and other physician extenders.[23]

Also, *immediate attention must be given to building a cadre of technical and administrative staff at the central and decentralized levels of the MSPP, with skills in developing policies, planning, and providing oversight.* Top management at the MSPP has shown leadership and administrative capability, particularly since the earthquake, but the layer of top management is thin and centralized in Port-au-Prince. *The MSPP needs to build middle- and lower-level management capability. Much of the training required to achieve this could be provided through donor-funded technical assistance.*

Capacity-building at the central level should focus on policy development and national-level planning and oversight. Capacity-building at the departmental level should focus on service contract oversight and progress and quality monitoring within the department, as well as budget management. Capacity-building at the commune level should focus on fostering community involvement in service delivery, particularly with respect to promoting the effective use of community health workers—individuals who are chosen by their communities to provide basic health and medical services in the absence of or to supplement professional health workers.

---

[23] A trained health professional who provides quasi-autonomous health care under a particular physician's license and supervision, including physician assistants, nurse-midwives, nurse practitioners, and other allied health professionals.

Although it is important to rebuild training institutions for health-care professionals to develop a workforce that meets Haiti's needs, results take years, and the numbers trained will remain relatively small. *A more immediate and pervasive response to unmet demand for health services would be to expand the use of Haiti's community health workers.* The use of these workers for health promotion and disease prevention has been an effective means for extending the reach of health systems in fragile and conflict-affected states. Community health workers can provide health education (e.g., family planning, nutrition), as well as preventive and (limited) treatment services. They can also play a role in improving the collection and reporting of health and population data (e.g., tracking births and incidence of communicable disease). Their use is particularly appealing in Haiti because of the lack of access to care, the number of health and population problems stemming from a lack of basic health education and preventive services, the excess mortality linked to communicable disease, and lack of civic involvement.

The community health–worker model has already been successfully utilized in several rural areas of Haiti (using community health agents), but its use is neither widespread nor supported by the public health system. *Use of NGO-contracted or volunteer community health workers could be made part of the contracting requirements for the delivery of health services in each area of Haiti, and the MSPP could develop guidelines on what services community health workers can provide and on their training.*

Examine Health-Care Financing Options

Although Haiti has relied heavily on donor aid to finance the health system, such an approach is not sustainable and does not provide predictability. Although donor funding will continue to be required over the next three to five years, and probably much longer, steps should be taken now to lay the foundation for a sustainable financing structure for Haiti's health sector.

The MSPP's current interim plan recognizes the need to address health-care financing and suggests creating a new funding model and providing free care for certain segments of the population. The *Vision and Roadmap for Haiti* recommends creating a health-insurance scheme for all Haitians. It suggests Rwanda's *mutuelles* (community insurance) system as a good model. Before decisions are made, *the MSPP, with donor support, should contract a study to examine in detail the various options for financing the health-care system and model the implications of those options for access to care, health outcomes, and the continued viability of the system*. The study should examine switching from a cost-recovery model to a unitary cost model (one standard payment per visit), the use of sliding scales for various socioeconomic groups, offering free care nationwide for certain key programs determined critical to the well-being and development of Haiti (e.g., well care or primary care for children under five years of age), and the introduction of various types of insurance under different scenarios.

Haiti's health system may eventually be financed through a combination of government funds raised through tax revenues and individual payments, which could include insurance and direct payment of fees for services. Significant increases in government tax revenue will not be available in the time frame discussed here. However, studies on the best way to finance the sector should begin now, so that decisions can be made and related policies and programs put in place over the coming five years.

CHAPTER TEN

Donor Cooperation and Building the Haitian State

As the poorest country in the hemisphere, and the only country in the past three decades to see a long-term decline in GDP per capita, Haiti has been a focus of concern and interest for donors of humanitarian and development assistance for two generations. The United States has been the largest bilateral donor of humanitarian and development assistance every year since 1990, contributing between one-quarter and half of all official flows to Haiti, followed by Canada and the European Union. Multilateral donors provide much of the remainder, led by the IDB and the World Bank. In the 19 years between 1990 and 2008, official donors disbursed $6.9 billion to Haiti, of which $911 million was disbursed in 2008 alone (Figure 10.1).[1] Despite this major commitment of resources, Haiti's economic, social, and political situations have worsened.

One explanation for this failure is that, while large in the aggregate, on a year-to-year basis, donor engagement and assistance funding have varied widely in response to Haitian political developments. When adverse political events took place, donors often sharply limited the share of development assistance channeled through the Haitian state, sometimes circumventing the state altogether, supporting NGOs and using implementing partners instead. Donors reasoned that it was counterproductive to strengthen state institutions when the state was

[1] Disbursement data as reported to the OECD Development Assistance Committee (DAC) (OECD, undated [b]). In addition, since 2004, UN member states have been funding MINUSTAH, with assessed funding for the fiscal year July 2009–June 2010 set at $611 million, including $3 million of "quick impact" development projects.

Figure 10.1
Official Development-Assistance Disbursements to Haiti, 2008 (millions of dollars)

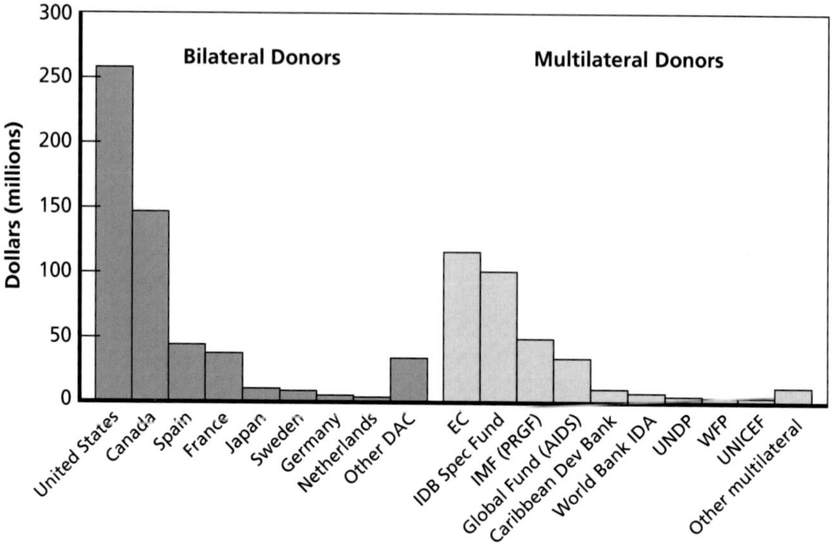

SOURCE: OECD (undated [b]).
NOTE: DAC = Development Assistance Committee. EC = European Commission. PRGF = Poverty Reduction and Growth Facility. AIDS = acquired immunodeficiency syndrome. IDA = International Development Association. UNDP = United Nations Development Programme. WFP = World Food Programme.
RAND *MG1039-10.1*

acting in nondemocratic and repressive ways. Yet, as a result, the weakened Haitian state was that much less capable of pursuing objectives to foster economic growth and protect society from crime, disease, and hunger.

Since 2004, in response to visible improvements in Haiti's political stability, and consistent with agreed international models, such as the *Paris Declaration on Aid Effectiveness*,[2] donors progressively worked in partnership with the Haitian state. Donors have sought to involve state institutions and civil society in the formulation of strategies and setting priorities.

---

[2] High Level Forum on Aid Effectiveness (2005).

Bilateral and multilateral agencies have varied in the degree to which they coordinate with each other. Several donors are involved in each sector. Differences in perspectives, rivalries, and competition for leadership exist at the donor level and among implementing NGOs and other institutions. Some Haitian government officials welcome the overlapping assistance efforts, which they feel result in more resources for the country and offer more choice of approaches.

The January 12 earthquake has brought both a quantum increase in resources and unprecedented attention to the international effort to assist Haiti, while gravely aggravating Haiti's immediate housing, health, environmental, and other problems. Donors have effectively coordinated postearthquake humanitarian assistance in accordance with international best practices. In the first days after the earthquake, the Haitian government ceased to function, but it has since become a partner with growing influence in directing humanitarian relief.

This chapter describes the development of relations between donors and the Haitian government since the January 12 earthquake and appraises the new architecture for allocating assistance agreed at the March 31, 2010, international donors' conference. It concludes with our recommendations for improving the effectiveness of donor engagement with the Haitian state and for better cooperation among donors.

The Challenges

The first priority for donors after the earthquake was humanitarian relief. Assistance agencies and NGOs already present in country—working with the government of Haiti, MINUSTAH, and international agencies—mobilized to rescue those trapped by collapsed buildings and to provide immediate medical care for the badly injured. Within 24 hours, advance elements of U.S. Marines and Army rescue teams were arriving in country to help MINUSTAH with security; the U.S. Navy hospital ship USNS *Comfort* was under way to Haiti shortly thereafter.

Many acute challenges affected short-term donor and NGO cooperation with the government of Haiti. The National Palace had collapsed, as had most ministry buildings, including the Ministry of Economy and Finance, MJSP, and the headquarters of the HNP. The five-story UN country team headquarters building also was destroyed, with the loss of more than 100 UN staffers, including Special Representative of the Secretary-General (SRSG) Hédi Annabi. Humanitarian agencies and NGOs lost key staffers. The Port-au-Prince airport terminal building and tower were badly damaged and unusable, as were piers at the state-owned container port.

U.S. military flight controllers, with Haitian government concurrence, took over flight operations at the airport to deconflict flight clearances and maximize runway and ramp utilization. The Dominican Republic offered its airports and seaports for the rapid transshipment of supplies.

The official Haitian government estimate is that more than 300,000 Haitians are dead and total damages exceed $8 billion.[3] Roughly 1.2 million Haitians, 12 percent of the population, are now housed in temporary and emergency shelters.[4] The value of destroyed physical assets (e.g., housing, schools, hospitals, roads, bridges, ports, airports) was estimated at $4.3 billion, and the effect on economic flows (e.g., production losses, lost employment) at $3.6 billion.

With extensive international help, the Haitian state began to function again after several days, with the HNP (fortunately) generally considered to be the first Haitian government entity to reestablish an effective presence in the badly damaged capital and major cities of the south.[5] The UN sent a new acting SRSG and moved quickly to bring temporary officials from other UN offices around the world. UN agencies based their operations in tents and temporary structures on the UN logistics base near the airport.

In accordance with established best practices from recent complex emergencies and natural disasters, the UN Office for the Coordination of Humanitarian Affairs (OCHA) established 12 "clusters" to coordinate Haitian and international donor and NGO humanitar-

---

3 Republic of Haiti (2010a, p. 7).

4 Inter-Agency Standing Committee (2010).

5 Booth (2010).

ian responses. The World Bank, USAID, CIDA, and the European Union have also been involved, as have many of the major NGOs (e.g., CARE, Partners in Health, Médecins sans Frontières, Catholic Relief Services, World Vision, the International Committee of the Red Cross [ICRC]). In addition to coordinating and deconflicting operations in a very difficult environment, several of the clusters have done outstanding jobs in collating and sharing information among donors, humanitarian NGOs, and the Haitian government, primarily using the Internet.[6]

As the emergency and humanitarian phase of the response took shape, donors and the Haitian government began to look at the daunting task of reconstruction, adopting the slogan "building back better." The Canadian government hosted a ministerial meeting of donors and international agencies on January 25, 2010, at which agreement was reached to conduct a PDNA to inform the Haitian government's *Action Plan for National Recovery and Development of Haiti*. The UN agreed to convene a postdisaster donors' conference in New York on March 31, 2010, to review these documents, coordinate the international response, and assemble new pledges for meeting the requirements.

With technical help from McKinsey and Company, the Haitian government led the PDNA effort and the subsequent month-long process to update the national development plan to estimate the financial requirements and determine the strategies needed to build back better. Focus-group and outreach meetings were held with Haitian citizens,[7] the Haitian private sector,[8] the Haitian diaspora,[9] MINUSTAH

---

[6] For example, see Logistics Cluster (undated), Inter-Agency Standing Committee (2010), or CCCM Cluster Haiti (undated).

[7] Office of the UN Special Envoy for Haiti (undated).

[8] Hosted on March 15 by the IDB in Port-au-Prince. The Haitian Private Sector Economic Forum (2010) submitted a paper titled *Vision and Roadmap for Haiti*.

[9] OAS (2010).

stakeholders,[10] local-government authorities in Haiti,[11] and international NGOs and implementing partners.[12]

The resulting *Action Plan for National Recovery and Development of Haiti* set out a vision for reconstruction in four areas: territorial (planning new development areas and associated infrastructure), economic (developing agriculture and manufacturing sectors), social (health and education), and institutional (making state institutions viable). The action plan envisaged three phases of operations: the emergency period, the implementation period (18 months from the earthquake), and the subsequent ten years. The total requested for the implementation period is $5.8 billion, along with an additional $3.8 billion during the rest of the ensuing decade. Of $5.8 billion in short-term assistance, $350 million is sought for budgetary support for the 18 months through the end of 2011. These were the numbers put before the March 31, 2010, donors' conference.

The action plan presented a new-to-Haiti architecture for managing such large flows of funds. A key element was agreement to establish a short-term joint Haitian government and donor commission to oversee the effort, now called the Interim Haiti Recovery Commission (IHRC). The action plan envisages an IHRC that "gives its approval to project proposals assessed according to the extent to which they comply with and are coordinated with" the Haiti development plan, "prepares and seeks out projects compatible" with the priorities of the plan, and "decides on the admissibility of external submissions."[13]

The IHRC has a complicated decisionmaking structure. It is cochaired by the prime minister of Haiti and an eminent foreign figure

---

[10] Organized by the government of Brazil; the government of Haiti sponsored the outreach meeting with MINUSTAH's stakeholders held in New York on March 23.

[11] Hosted by France on March 23 in Martinique.

[12] Hosted in New York on March 25 by the Office of the Special Envoy. At the meeting, InterAction, a grouping of U.S. NGOs and implementing partners, submitted a memorandum titled *From the Ground Up: InterAction Member Recommendations on Recovery and Reconstruction in Haiti* (InterAction, 2010), emphasizing, among other things, that reconstruction should be mindful of social equity, women and children, and civil-society organizations.

[13] Republic of Haiti (2010a, p. 54).

(former U.S. President Bill Clinton)[14] and has government, parliamentary, and nongovernmental Haitian members, as well as representatives from the major international donors. The Haitian side has one more vote in the aggregate than foreigners; the president of Haiti must confirm all decisions in order for them to be executed.

After 18 months (the period for which it is anticipated major international reconstruction funding will be committed), the IHRC will convert into an ongoing Haitian Development Authority (HDA) without a foreign decisionmaking role.

In addition, in the action plan, the government of Haiti requested that a multidonor trust fund (MDTF) be established for donors to pool their contributions, reduce overlap, and simplify management and administration.[15] After some debate, the Haitian government and major donors decided that the World Bank's IDA would be the trustee for the fund.[16]

In the final communiqué of the donors' conference, participants agreed to support the Haitian government's reconstruction plan and to align their assistance with it and "welcomed" the establishment of the IHRC and the HDA, which would "ensure leadership by the Haitian government in establishing priorities for international assistance and in coordinating, expediting and implementing that assistance." A final sentence commits the participants to simultaneously assist "in building the administrative capacity of the Haitian government."[17] These communiqué sentences reflect the state-building dilemmas Haiti faces. On the one hand, the IHRC will allow the Haitian government to engage with the donors on priorities and, through the secretariat, will give it the technical expertise to do so effectively. On the other hand, the creation of the IHRC and the HDA may well further erode the responsibilities and authorities of responsible Haitian ministries.

---

[14] At the international donors' conference, it was announced that former President Bill Clinton would play this cochair role.

[15] Republic of Haiti (2010a, p. 55).

[16] Discussion with senior Ministry of Economy and Finance official, Port-au-Prince, April 2010.

[17] International Donors' Conference Towards a New Future for Haiti (2010, ¶7).

Finally—and most importantly—the donor community pledged funds in support of the Haitian government's requests and in support of the new assistance-management architecture. In all, 59 donors pledged $9.9 billion at the conference, with $5.4 billion to be available for use in the 18 months through 2011.[18] Of the $9.9 billion total, donors also announced their intention to channel $5.26 billion through the MDTF. (In its supplemental request to Congress, the U.S. administration requested authority to contribute up to $120 million to the MDTF.)

Appraisal of Donor Cooperation with Haitian State Institutions

Much is going right in the international effort to support state-building in Haiti. There is widespread agreement that the international community should apply lessons learned from the generally successful effort to rebuild the Indonesian province of Aceh after the devastation of the 2004 tsunami (see "Lessons from Aceh").

Donors with long experience in Haiti seem to appreciate the costs of the "light-switch" assistance efforts of the 1990s, when assistance efforts were abruptly stopped after political upheavals and coups, only to be restarted slowly and with difficulty when a legitimate government was restored. Use of NGOs and implementing partners allowed humanitarian efforts to continue in these periods but with little Haitian government input or oversight, undermining the Haitian government's capacity to perform these basic governmental tasks.

It has helped greatly that, since 2004, Haiti's security situation stabilized through the commitment of MINUSTAH forces. Not coincidentally, the most successful state-building effort thus far has been building the HNP, supported by MINUSTAH, the United States, and other donors. The HNP was among the first Haitian institutions to resume operations after the earthquake, although rigid distinctions between security and development-assistance funding streams among

---

[18] As reported in the pledge listing spreadsheet (Haiti Reconstruction Platform, undated).

Lessons from Aceh

In establishing an MDTF and a national development commission, donors and the Haitian government sought to adapt mechanisms used in the Aceh tsunami reconstruction effort. The December 26, 2004, earthquake and subsequent tsunami caused widespread destruction throughout the population centers on the west coast of the Indonesian province of Aceh on the island of Sumatra. On January 19, 2005, the Indonesian government, with the help of the UN and other donors, completed a preliminary damage and loss assessment report, estimating damages and losses equal to $2.3 billion.[a] The president of Indonesia appointed a personally trusted, experienced leader to coordinate reconstruction and established a special agency to manage reconstruction in cooperation with donors. A major effort was made to involve communities in rebuilding decisions. International donors pooled $700 million into a World Bank–administered MDTF.[b]

In a 2006 report that drew lessons from the reconstruction effort, former president Clinton urged the following substantive priorities for organizers of future such efforts:[c] (1) Families and communities should drive their own recovery. (2) Recovery should promote fairness and equity. (3) Donors should empower local governments to manage recovery and to strengthen government institutions engaged in recovery. (4) Financial accountability is critical to ensuring ongoing donor support. (5) Good recovery planning and coordination depend on good information. (6) The UN and World Bank need to clarify their respective roles early in the process. (7) The expanding role of NGOs carries greater responsibilities for quality control in recovery efforts. (8) Governments and aid agencies need to create the conditions for entrepreneurs to flourish. (9) Agency partnerships ought to be the norm, rather than rivalry and unhealthy competition. (10) Recovery should reduce risks and build resilience against future disasters.

There have been other studies of the Aceh experience. A CIDA conference drew attention to the debate in Aceh as to whether donors should build transitional shelters or go directly to construction of permanent ones, and recounted the tensions between local NGOs and international agencies when the agencies sought to hire local NGO staffers.[d] A comprehensive study sponsored by the UK Disasters Emergency Committee (DEC) also emphasized community involvement and highlighted the difficulties involved in design choices for replacement housing. It noted that some early structures had to be demolished because they did not meet seismic standards. The DEC study also found that large-scale shelter-construction efforts were difficult for many NGOs, which did not have in-house expertise in design and construction oversight.[e]

A study of the tsunami assistance efforts of six major NGOs by Grantmakers Without Borders identified some of the forces *against* effective cooperation: competition among implementing NGOs for donor dollars and expert staff; the tension between the perceived need for immediate action and the time it takes for community involvement; conflicting philosophies between NGOs, the private sector, and social-justice movements; and the pressure from media outlets that alternatively extol and excoriate aid agencies and NGOs.[f]

[a] World Bank (undated [a]). [b] Von Amsberg (2010). Von Amsberg is the World Bank's country director for Indonesia. [c] Office of the UN Special Envoy for Haiti (2006). See also Office of the UN Special Envoy for Haiti (undated). [d] CIDA (2007). [e] Da Silva (2010, p. 77). [f] Roper (2006, p. 20).

donors hobbled worthwhile initiatives, such as establishing HNP posts in camps for victims of the earthquake.[19]

Donors have learned to work with the Haitian government in fashioning overarching strategies to tackle Haiti's daunting problems. The experiences of working out the ICF in 2004, the national GPRSP of 2007, and *Haiti: A New Paradigm* in 2009[20] were useful to the work on the PDNA and the *Action Plan for National Recovery and Development of Haiti*, both completed under tight time pressure in March 2010. The World Bank–supported financial management information system is starting to come online in the Ministry of Finance, although it was hampered by the collapse of the Ministry of Finance's buildings and is available to buttress the Haitian government's case for immediate budgetary support. Donors have also worked with the Haitian government to devise separate and transparent executing units to undertake projects outside of the normal ministry mechanisms.[21]

Yet, in some respects, donor cooperation is a tough sell. In Port-au-Prince, we asked senior Haitian government officials who dealt with many donors supporting overlapping projects (for public-administration reform, police training, and financial management) whether they would find it more efficient to work with only one lead donor in a subject area. The Haitian reaction was consistently negative: Even though multiple donor and NGO programs impose major burdens in terms of administrative compliance, our Haitian interlocutors believed that they obtained more support and had more options with many competing donors.

Even though the global economy is struggling, Haiti is benefiting from special preferences in the U.S. market through the HOPE II program. Congressional committees have reportedly agreed to triple quota

---

[19] We have been told that humanitarian-relief agencies did not respond fully to HNP requests for tents and equipment to establish permanent posts in the tent camps. In the case of USAID, statutory prohibitions on use of development assistance for security purposes would not allow for such contributions (discussion with HNP official, Port-au-Prince, April 23, 2010).

[20] *Haiti: A New Paradigm* (2009).

[21] One senior Ministry of Economy and Finance official told us that there were 20 such special executing units established in recent years for IDB projects alone.

volumes following the earthquake, as was requested by former presidents Bill Clinton and George W. Bush.[22] Such an enlarged HOPE II quota would help Haiti attract new investments in apparel factories, especially if Haiti tackles constraints related to transportation, housing, and doing business.

Recommendations

Effective donor cooperation in support of state-building and recovery in Haiti faces special challenges. Haiti's troubled history, deep poverty, environmental destruction, recent natural disasters, and unresolved political tensions make state-building and economic development especially difficult. There is little scope—or time—for donor competition or disagreement. Priorities must be set. Accordingly, our recommendations are aimed at making the IHRC and MDTF function effectively, helping the United States play the leadership role it must, and harnessing the power of NGOs and Haitian communities.

Make the Interim Haiti Recovery Commission an Effective Decisionmaking Body

The most urgent priority is to stand up the IHRC. At this writing, several months after the international donors' conference, the Haitian government decree establishing the IHRC has not been promulgated, and an executive director has not been chosen. Once these steps are taken, there will inevitably be a delay until the commission is functional and able to fulfill its coordination and approval responsibilities. It will also be a challenge for the Haitian government to staff the IHRC secretariat without drawing away scarce skilled staff from line ministries.

The purpose of the IHRC is to provide the expertise and capacity to realize Haitian leadership of the recovery effort. It also is designed to institute systems of accountability and transparency. In the short term, donor support for the IHRC and the creation of a special status for Haitian personnel on it can help the Haitian state attract the best and

---

22 "House, Senate Panel Leaders Unveil Haiti Preferences Deal" (2010).

brightest Haitians back from the NGO and donor sectors and from the diaspora. Many Haitians, however, are concerned lest the IHRC drain talent and responsibility from the mainline ministries, which, at the end of the day, have to deliver services and good governance to Haiti. *To balance these priorities, the IHRC must remain limited in scale (a secretariat of 100 or fewer) and coordinate with and fully utilize Haitian ministries' capabilities. Moreover, donors should second top-flight technical staff to the IHRC, and such officials should also have a training mandate, given the short life span of the commission. The goal should be to have a capable Haitian professional cadre ready to take over operations (as the HDA) within 24 months.*

An early test of the value and clout of the IHRC will be the willingness of major bilateral donors—especially USAID and CIDA—to coordinate their programs through it and to adapt them in light of IHRC input. *Major donors, including the United States, should submit all project and program concepts to the IHRC for coordination and be willing to adapt them in accordance with Haitian and other donors' plans and preferences.*

Scarce Haitian and donor resources should not be wasted on small-scale, duplicative, or overlapping pilot projects, even if the Haitians are reluctant to give them up and donors prefer them so as to minimize the risk of failure. Better to do a small number of big things comprehensively and well. *Such an outcome requires donor specialization. The IHRC will have to lean against tendencies toward letting donors do only what they wish and must be willing to say "no," if only in order to say "yes" to the assistance projects that matter.*

Decisionmaking by the IHRC will be important. *Donors and the Haitian government should adopt a consensus decisionmaking model for the IHRC to set priorities and coordinate efforts, backed up by rigorous cost-benefit analysis.* Programs should be considered sector by sector, and sign-off on tasks and responsibilities should be by the Haitian government and all major donors.

Monitoring and evaluation (M&E) are even more important in the recovery phase than they are for the humanitarian phase. Assistance partners and Haitian government agencies will be driven by what can be tracked and measured. *Design of M&E components of programs must be a responsibility of the IHRC from the outset and should be harmonized with donor needs so that donors, the MDTF, and the IHRC all track the same indicators and read the same evaluation reports.*

Donors and the IHRC also need to be mindful of economic incentives in the design of recovery strategies. Consistent with the lessons from tsunami recovery, Haitians will do much on their own to reconstruct their homes and build their economy, if the incentives are right. Free food and medical care in the camps, put in place for humanitarian reasons in the earthquake aftermath, serve as incentives to increase the populations of tent camps in unsustainable ways. *It should be a donor and NGO priority to find new means of offering social protection in ways that support transition.*

To the extent that the IHRC succeeds in setting priorities and standards, donors may react adversely. In particular, legislatures (such as the U.S. Congress) may respond by earmarking even more of the assistance budget for sectors or delivery modes that the IHRC does not consider priorities. NGOs denied a high-profile role in a sector that eases fund-raising may curtail their activities or withdraw from Haiti. Choices are not cost-free, but the major lesson of Aceh is the importance of meaningful host country–donor coordination.

Finally, donors should be alert to indications that the Haitian government seeks to use assistance funding to serve partisan political interests or the dominance of elite groups, and should raise these issues in the IHRC and otherwise as needed at an early stage.

Strongly Support the Multidonor Trust Fund

The World Bank–led MDTF must become operational quickly. Setting up a trust fund took more than a year in the Aceh case. For the IHRC to have credibility and impact, it will need access to the resources of the MDTF, and it will need it quickly. It is striking that the United States, which, for several years, contributed 40 percent of official flows to Haiti, is requesting congressional authorization to contribute only up to $120 million to the MDTF, just over 2 percent of the total resources pledged to the MDTF. *The United States will not have influence in the MDTF commensurate with its contributions to Haiti in general unless it substantially increases its commitment to the fund. More broadly, we rec-*

ommend that every official donor in Haiti channel at least 10 percent of official flows through the MDTF, since the fund can support state-building activities most efficiently.

But, even with greater resources, *the MDTF should be used principally to finance activities on a scale or in a sector that cannot otherwise attract donor or NGO support.* Use of the MDTF for a program that could otherwise receive multilateral or bilateral donor finance (or NGO self-finance) would be a waste of resources.

Encourage Nongovernmental Organizations to Support State-Building

International NGOs, which remain significant sources of expertise for Haiti, now have substantial funds from the outpouring of contributions from around the world. They should make contributions to building the Haitian state, toward the long-term goal of eliminating Haiti's need for their support. *Thus, self-funded NGOs should be expected either to make grants equal to 10 percent of their program funds to the Haitian state, including for budget support, as recommended by President Clinton,*[23] *or to pay customs duties on their imported vehicles and supplies. NGOs also should be required to withhold regular Haitian payroll and income taxes for their Haitian and expatriate staff.*

Moreover, *NGOs with a self-financed budget in Haiti of more than $10 million should be required to present their plans and activities to the IHRC for coordination with government- and donor-funded activities in the same sector.* The self-funded NGOs should also benefit from understanding and cooperation with other activities in their fields of endeavor.

Facilitate Community Involvement and Information Flow

Study of other state-building efforts has shown the value of community involvement to broaden the base of support and to ensure cultural and political acceptability of reconstruction efforts. Donors now accept the need to seek community buy-in for projects and assistance programs. *Sustainability will require that community involvement be more than epi-*

[23] Gross (2010), quoted in International Crisis Group (2010, fn. 120).

sodic consultations when major plans are devised. Community involvement should be ongoing and supported by information flows in both directions. Haitians need to know what is planned for their communities and have an opportunity to contribute to project conceptualization and project design. This is especially true for the homeless and displaced and will improve the legitimacy of the Haitian government in domestic public opinion.

With World Bank support, the Haitian government has established the Haiti Reconstruction Platform Internet site, but it is as yet at a high level of generality. *The website should be loaded with much more in the way of investment project specifics. Signage should be developed and consistently used to identify public works funded by the MDTF and other donors. The Haitian government should also build public confidence by offering full transparency of Haitian public-sector employee totals, audit mechanisms, and results. For their part, donors need to offer the Haitian government more transparency in their planning.*

Appoint a Senior Coordinator for U.S. Policy and Assistance Programs

In support of a strong, sustained international effort to help Haiti overcome its history and the manifold constraints it faces to recovery and development, the United States and other donors will need to make changes as well. A prerequisite for better cooperation among donors will be better coordination within the U.S. government, which, in turn, would allow the United States to more effectively influence other donors. *As in the Balkans during the 1990s and with respect to Afghanistan/Pakistan policy now, the coherence of U.S. policy would be enhanced by the appointment of a full-time, high-level coordinator* (or envoy) with the rank and access to consult with President Préval and oversee the Haitian assistance budgets and policies of USAID, the State Department, Treasury, Agriculture, Homeland Security, and other U.S. government agencies with programs in Haiti.

In order to make donor coordination truly effective, and in support of UN Special Envoy and IHRC cochair Clinton, such a senior U.S. government coordinator should *underpin the formal donor-coordination process with an informal and behind-the-scenes "friends of Haiti" small group of the largest bilateral and multilateral donors (e.g., U.S., Canada, the EU, France, the IDB, and the World Bank).*

Exercise Donor Leverage

There is no purely programmatic solution to many of the problems identified in this report. No amount of training, advising, capacity-building, and facilitative assistance will secure enough support within the Haitian political establishment to achieve the necessary changes. *Only politics, not programs, will lead to reform on the necessary scale.*

Over the next 18 months, donors are projected to contribute $5.4 billion to Haiti, equivalent to 57 percent of Haiti's GDP for this period, as projected by the IMF. Of the total amount pledged to Haiti, the top five donors (Venezuela, the IDB, the United States, the European Union, and Spain) account for more than two-thirds of this total. *In principle, these donors should have a substantial amount of influence on the political process. This leverage will produce results, however, only if it is exercised in a calculated, if also very discreet, careful, and sensitive fashion.*

Donors know how their own governments work. People elect representatives whose future depends on delivering patronage and projects to their constituents. Special-interest groups also feed at the public trough and influence decisionmaking. Anyone seeking to effect meaningful reform has to work within this system of pork-barrel politics, building constituencies one member, one contribution, and one vote at a time. Why should donors expect any more-enlightened behavior from Haiti's politicians than they experience with their own?

Yet, aid bureaucracies are strongly averse to playing politics. They vigorously resist interference from the policy wings of their own foreign ministries. They are horrified at the thought of development money being spent to grease the recipient countries' political wheels, an attitude in which they are reinforced by their own parliaments, whose members are all too aware of how that game is played. Development doctrine stresses the importance of indigenous "ownership" but fails to put corresponding emphasis on the degree of salesmanship needed to sell the prospective owner on the new purchase. These inhibitions will need to be overcome if international assistance to Haiti is to have any more-enduring impact for the good in the future than it has had in the past.

CHAPTER ELEVEN

Conclusion

Hope for a more prosperous and peaceful future for the Haitian people lies in building a more effective and resilient state. The discussions herein of challenges have shown that Haitian state institutions are riddled with weaknesses in the areas of human resources, organization, procedures, and policies. As a result of these weaknesses, the state, on its own, has been incapable of providing security for the Haitian people, ensuring justice, promoting economic growth, or delivering public services. The appraisals of reform plans and initiatives in this report suggest that devising lists of measures needed to repair the state's weaknesses is relatively easy but that formulating strategies to address those weaknesses is hard—and implementation is even harder.

None of the principal pre- and postearthquake planning documents[1] sets out a fully elaborated strategy for strengthening Haiti's state institutions, nor collectively do the sectoral documents discussed in the preceding chapters. This report aims to support the development of a Haitian state-building strategy by recommending how to build on existing plans for improving institutions and the delivery of public services. It focuses on suggesting priorities for state-building, taking into account the effects of the January 2010 earthquake.

[1] For example, the GPRSP, the framework program (Republic of Haiti, 2007), and the *Action Plan for National Recovery and Development of Haiti* (Republic of Haiti, 2010a).

Strategic Framework

Formulating a state-building strategy first requires identifying the state's core functions. The strategy should articulate the means for developing the state's capacity to perform those functions efficiently and in ways that serve the public's interests. The selection of functions on which this report focuses is not meant to suggest that other functions are unimportant, but it represents an effort to address those that are essential to moving Haiti toward greater stability, economic growth, and improvements in social well-being in the next three to five years.

We have addressed public administration because effective bureaucratic institutions with well-qualified personnel, sound procedures, and adequate infrastructure are the backbone of the state. Many of those in Port-au-Prince with whom we consulted in preparing this report commented on the lack of *systems* in Haiti (for example, while there are education providers, there is no *education system* of which to speak). Developing a sound public administration is crucial to instituting a more systematic approach to governance.

Justice and policing are core functions of the state because they are essential to promoting stability—a prerequisite for improvements in many other areas. Growth-oriented economic policies and infrastructure development and management are among the chief concerns of the state because they are vital to lifting the Haitian people out of poverty. Ensuring the provision of accessible and reasonably high-quality education and health care are core functions as well because these services are essential to the population's well-being. In addition, improved availability of these services would help keep more of the middle class in Haiti, thus raising the skill level of the workforce.

Priorities

After winnowing the state's functions to the most-essential ones, development of a state-building strategy requires establishing priorities. The plans and proposals appraised in this report are, in general, too broad in scope and too ambitious in their objectives and fail to set priorities or lay out a sequence for introducing changes. Many do not set timelines based on considered estimates of the time needed to introduce and implement the various steps in the proposed programs. In most instances, benchmarks based on targeted outcomes are lacking. At times, plans fail to identify who is responsible for implementing actions. The more-elaborately detailed plans—such as the framework program[2]—provide a good foundation for further, more-strategic planning, however.

Plans that do not set priorities and detail sequencing and responsibilities are unlikely to have much effect on government policymaking and donor funding decisions. If priorities are not set, the government's ability to carry out any plans is compromised. And broad plans with an abundance of objectives enable donors to justify whatever projects they wish to fund, leading to incoherent donor interventions.

In the aftermath of the January 12 earthquake, setting priorities has become even more important. No government could successfully manage *simultaneously* and within a few years to thoroughly remake itself, pursue radical decentralization, prepare and adopt major legislation in many areas, spur economic growth, guarantee access to justice where there has been none, amend a constitution, organize housing solutions for hundreds of thousands of people, and refashion the provision of basic services—yet, all of these objectives and many others have been embraced in the notion of "building back better."

Determining state-building priorities calls for considering what is necessary, feasible, and sustainable by the Haitian government over the long term. The latter is important in light of the many examples of projects that ended as soon as donor funding ended, or—like some donor-funded infrastructure—deteriorated because no provision was made for maintenance when the project was built.

In Chapter One, we argue that priorities must be fiscally sustainable; commensurate with the administrative capacity of the Haitian government; realistic in their prospects for implementation; geared toward enhancing the effectiveness of the Haitian state; and coherent. Using these criteria and drawing on the analysis in the preceding chap-

---

2 Republic of Haiti (2007).

ters, we have selected a set of changes that we believe are of the highest priority and, collectively, are realistic and manageable. These changes stand out as meriting the greatest degree of political and policy attention by the government of Haiti and donors, as well as full funding.

First, providing public security must remain at the forefront. Civil unrest could quickly stall and even reverse state-building and reconstruction activities. Given Haiti's history of episodic violence and extraconstitutional changes of government, there is no room for complacency on this front. Until Haiti's own security forces are capable of handling any likely outbreak of violence, UN peacekeepers will continue to be needed. The government of Haiti and the United Nations should agree to keep an international military and police force in Haiti for at least the next five years and to diminish it only gradually thereafter. Second, for police reform to fully take hold, the judiciary and corrections system will have to be substantially improved. In particular, the procedural and communication links among police, prosecutors, judges, and prisons urgently need strengthening. The Haitian government also should create a special pretrial detainee review mechanism to resolve the huge number of cases of illegally prolonged detention. Donors and the Haitian government should prioritize judicial reform even over continued efforts to build up the police.

The Haitian government, with donor support, should also focus on establishing a property-dispute resolution mechanism, which would address an urgent set of issues and would directly benefit many Haitians. Putting in place an accelerated procedure for determining asset ownership is essential to reducing obstacles to reconstruction and economic activity. In conjunction with this, work that is under way to address serious gaps in birth, death, and identity registration should be completed expeditiously.

Third, because improvements in public administration are vital to fortifying the state against future crises, funding and technical assistance for reform measures in this area are of utmost importance even amid a proliferation of other needs and priorities. Funding for public-administration reform should not be diverted to the understandably desirable and expensive construction of buildings to house the government. A particularly crucial priority is civil service reform, which would include creating job descriptions, standards and procedures for hiring and firing, a merit promotion system, salary grades, and performance incentives.

Fourth, the Haitian government, together with the donor community, should accelerate removal of rubble on a nondiscriminatory basis. This is the single most important step toward reconstruction that the Haitian government and donors can take. The vast quantities of rubble in Port-au-Prince and other earthquake-affected areas forestall reconstruction and economic recovery. The continued presence of rubble also undermines public confidence in the government, limiting its scope for making difficult political choices.

Fifth, to accelerate economic growth, the Haitian government should quickly eliminate unnecessary procedures involved in registering businesses and property and reduce the cost and length of time needed to complete the remaining steps. To ensure that the electric-power and other utilities are available for businesses and households, the Haitian government should move to full cost-recovery pricing for electric power and decentralize and enforce collection of bills owed.

Sixth, the role of the state in delivery of education and health services should be better focused—that is, both strengthened and narrowed. The objective should be to create and implement a feasible model of governance in these sectors. Specifically, the state should concentrate on establishing policies concerning where and how services are provided, setting quality standards, creating rules that promote access, and carrying out monitoring and enforcement actions. For the near to medium term, government and donor efforts will be better spent on developing these administrative and regulatory capabilities than on expanding the currently very limited direct government provision of services.

For the health sector, this means that consideration should be given to shifting the operation of all health centers and hospitals to NGOs and other private institutions. The government, with donor technical and funding assistance, could establish a performance-based contracting mechanism for the provision of health services throughout the country. For education, priority should be given to developing the skills of MENFP staff to enable them to regulate accredited schools and take action against those that do not meet reasonable standards.

Finally, throughout this report, we argue that donors need to strive for much more coherence among their programs, coordination of their interactions with the Haitian government, and collaboration with the government. Toward those ends, the government and donors should focus on making the IHRC an effective body. Major donors, most notably the United States, should submit all project and program concepts to the IHRC for coordination and be willing to adapt them in accordance with Haitian government and other donors' plans and preferences. If donors and the Haitian government do not use the IHRC to make decisions, the commission may become no more than an information exchange, and, if the largest donor, the United States, does not submit itself to this discipline, no one else will either.

Political Prerequisites

While this report has focused on practical steps that can be taken to strengthen Haitian state institutions, it should not be read as implying that state-building is a purely technical process. State-building is intimately connected with politics. Without executive decisiveness and legislative action, state-building cannot proceed. Thus, a considerable burden rests on the shoulders of Haiti's political leaders, who will need to rise to the challenge of overcoming a history of fractiousness, patronage, and indecision.

Donors have a role to play as well in promoting political consensus and encouraging adherence to strategic plans. In this regard, the United States, as the largest bilateral contributor, should better organize itself to engage politically with the government of Haiti through appointment of a full-time special coordinator or envoy with the rank necessary to consult with President Préval, UN Special Envoy and IHRC co-chair Clinton, and others on the international scene. Similarly, a handful of major bilateral and multilateral donors should organize themselves for more-coordinated political engagement with Haitian leaders through the creation of a "friends" or "contact" group for Haiti. Such a structure, working behind the scenes, could help to ensure the success of the IHRC.

Bibliography

Abdul Latif Jameel Poverty Action Lab, "Student Attendance," undated web page. As of July 14, 2010:
http://www.povertyactionlab.org/policy-lessons/education/student-attendance

Action plan—*See* Republic of Haiti (2010a).

Albrecht, Hans-Jörg, Louis Aucoin, and Vivienne M. O'Connor, *Building the Rule of Law in Haiti: New Laws for a New Era*, Washington, D.C.: U.S. Institute of Peace, August 2009. As of July 13, 2010:
http://library.usip.org/articles/1012481.1136/1.PDF

Allix, Grégoire, "Reconstruction d'Haïti: Le Casse-Tête de la Corruption," *Le Monde*, February 2, 2010, p. 4. As of July 13, 2010:
http://www.lemonde.fr/ameriques/article/2010/02/02/reconstruction-d-haiti-le-casse-tete-de-la-corruption_1300040_3222.html

Almond, Gabriel A., and Sidney Verba, *The Civic Culture: Political Attitudes and Democracy in Five Nations*, Princeton, N.J.: Princeton University Press, 1963.

Booth, William, "In a Turnabout, Police Are the Good Guys in Post-Quake Haiti," *Washington Post*, January 30, 2010. As of July 14, 2010:
http://www.washingtonpost.com/wp-dyn/content/article/2010/01/29/AR2010012904144.html

Buss, Terry F., *Why Foreign Aid to Haiti Failed*, Washington, D.C.: National Academy of Public Administration, 2006. As of July 13, 2010:
http://www.napawash.org/haiti_final.pdf

Buss, Terry F., with Adam Gardner, *Haiti in the Balance: Why Foreign Aid Has Failed and What We Can Do About It*, Washington, D.C.: Brookings Institution, 2008.

Call, Charles T., with Gigja Sorensen, *U.N. Peace Operations and State-Building: A Case Study of Haiti*, New York: Center on International Cooperation, New York University, May 2009. As of July 13, 2010:
http://www.cic.nyu.edu/peacebuilding/docs/haiti_call_sorensen.pdf

Canada's Civilian Reserve, *Police Capacity Building in Haiti: Lessons Learned and Best Practices from the CANADEM Deployment of Twenty Canadian Police Experts to Haiti*, Ottawa, 2009.

CANADEM—*See* Canada's Civilian Reserve.

Canadian International Development Agency, *Aid Effectiveness in the Transition from Disaster Relief to Reconstruction: Experiences from Asia*, modified April 7, 2007. As of July 14, 2010:
http://www.acdi-cida.gc.ca/acdi-cida/ACDI-CIDA.nsf/eng/RAC-12134015-PW8

Caroit, Jean-Michel, "L'ONU Est Critiquée pour Son Inaction Face aux Violences en Haïti," *Le Monde*, October 5, 2004.

Catalytic Fund, grant proposal summary, draft document, May 2010.

Cavallo, Eduardo A., Andrew Powell, and Oscar Becerra, *Estimating the Direct Economic Damage of the Earthquake in Haiti*, Washington, D.C.: Inter-American Development Bank, February 11, 2010. As of July 13, 2010:
http://idbdocs.iadb.org/wsdocs/getdocument.aspx?docnum=35072649

CCCM Cluster Haiti, undated home page. As of July 14, 2010:
http://groups.google.com/group/cccmhaiti

CCDPP—*See* Commission Consultative sur la Détention Préventive Prolongée.

CIDA—*See* Canadian International Development Agency.

Collier, Paul, *The Bottom Billion: Why the Poorest Countries Are Failing and What Can Be Done About It*, Oxford: Oxford University Press, 2007.

Collier, Paul, and Jean-Louis Warnholz, "Building Haiti's Economy, One Mango at a Time," *New York Times*, January 28, 2010. As of July 14, 2010:
http://www.nytimes.com/2010/01/29/opinion/29collier.html

Commission Consultative sur la Détention Préventive Prolongée, *Rapport Final sur la Problématique de la Détention Préventive Prolongée dans la Juridiction du Tribunal de Première Instance de Port-au-Prince*, Ministère de la Justice et de la Sécurité Publique, March 2008.

Constitution of the Republic of Haiti, 1987.

Da Silva, Jo, *Lessons from Aceh: Key Considerations in Post-Disaster Reconstruction*, Warwickshire, UK: Practical Action Publishing, 2010.

"Danish Minister Unhappy with EU's Slow Dispatch of Police to Haiti," *BBC Monitoring Europe*, January 27, 2010.

De Grauwe, Anton, *Without Capacity, There Is No Development: Rethinking Capacity Development*, Paris: United Nations Educational, Scientific and Cultural Organization, International Institute for Educational Planning, 2009.

Dobbins, James, Seth G. Jones, Keith Crane, and Beth Cole DeGrasse, *The Beginner's Guide to Nation-Building*, Santa Monica, Calif.: RAND Corporation, MG-557-SRF, 2007. As of July 14, 2010:
http://www.rand.org/pubs/monographs/MG557/

Dobbins, James, John G. McGinn, Keith Crane, Seth G. Jones, Rollie Lal, Andrew Rathmell, Rachel M. Swanger, and Anga R. Timilsina, *America's Role in Nation-Building: From Germany to Iraq*, Santa Monica, Calif.: RAND Corporation, MR-1753-RC, 2003. As of July 14, 2010:
http://www.rand.org/pubs/monograph_reports/MR1753/

Dolisca, Frito, Joshua M. McDaniel, Lawrence D. Teeter, and Curtis M. Jolly, "Land Tenure, Population Pressure, and Deforestation in Haiti: The Case of Forêt des Pins Reserve," *Journal of Forest Economics*, Vol. 13, No. 4, November 5, 2007, pp. 277–289.

Dorell, Orin, "More U.S. Military Personnel Head to Haiti for Relief Effort," *USA Today*, January 18, 2010. As of July 13, 2010:
http://www.usatoday.com/news/world/2010-01-17-us-steps-up-relief-effort_N.htm

DPKO—*See* United Nations Department of Peacekeeping Operations.

Duflo, Esther, Rema Hanna, and Stephen P. Ryan, *Incentives Work: Getting Teachers to Come to School*, Abdul Latif Jameel Poverty Action Lab, November 11, 2008. As of July 14, 2010:
http://www.povertyactionlab.org/sites/default/files/publications/
Incentives%20Work,%20Getting%20teachers%20to%20come%20to%20school.pdf

Duflo, Esther, Michael Kremer, and Pascaline Dupas, *Peer Effects, Pupil-Teacher Ratios, and Teacher Incentives in Kenya*, Innovations for Poverty Action, c. 2010. As of July 14, 2010:
http://www.povertyactionlab.org/evaluation/
peer-effects-pupil-teacher-ratios-and-teacher-incentives-kenya

Dziedzic, Michael, and Robert M. Perito, *Haiti: Confronting the Gangs of Port-au-Prince*, Washington, D.C.: U.S. Institute of Peace, September 2008. As of July 13, 2010:
http://www.usip.org/resources/haiti-confronting-the-gangs-port-au-prince

Eide, Eric, Dan Goldhaber, and Dominic Brewer, "The Teacher Labour Market and Teacher Quality," *Oxford Review of Economic Policy*, Vol. 20, No. 2, 2004, pp. 230–244.

Eizenstat, Stuart, John Edward Porter, and Jeremy Weinstein, "Rebuilding Weak States," *Foreign Affairs*, Vol. 84, No. 1, January–February 2005, pp. 134–146.

Environmental Performance Index, "Country Scores," undated web page. As of July 13, 2010:
http://epi.yale.edu/Countries

EPI—*See* Environmental Performance Index.

Erikson, Daniel P., "Haiti After Aristide: Still on the Brink," *Current History*, Vol. 104, No. 679, February 2005, pp. 83–90.

Fatton, Robert Jr., "The Impairments of Democratization: Haiti in Comparative Perspective," *Comparative Politics*, Vol. 31, No. 2, January 1999, pp. 209–229.

———, *Haiti's Predatory Republic: The Unending Transition to Democracy*, Boulder, Colo.: Lynne Reinner Publishers, 2002.

———, "Haiti: The Saturnalia of Emancipation and the Vicissitudes of Predatory Rule," *Third World Quarterly*, Vol. 27, No. 1, February 2006, pp. 115–133.

Fleury, Jean Sénat, *The Challenges of Judicial Reform in Haiti*, Hurah, 2007.

Foreign Affairs and International Trade Canada, "Canada's Contribution to Haiti: Four Years of Progress," modified January 22, 2010. As of July 13, 2010: http://www.international.gc.ca/start-gtsr/haiti-progress-progres-haiti.aspx

Fortin, Isabelle, and Yves-François Pierre, *Haïti et la Reforme de la Police Nationale d'Haïti*, North-South Institute, December 2008.

Framework program—*See* Republic of Haiti (2007).

GAO—*See* U.S. General Accounting Office.

Ghani, Ashraf, and Clare Lockhart, *Fixing Failed States: A Framework for Rebuilding a Fractured World*, Oxford: Oxford University Press, 2008.

Global Education Cluster, *Minutes from the Education Cluster Meeting: Strategic Group Meeting*, Port-au-Prince, May 4, 2010.

GPRSP—*See* Republic of Haiti (2008).

Gros, Jean-Germain, "Haiti's Flagging Transition," *Journal of Democracy*, Vol. 8, No. 4, 1997, pp. 94–109.

Gross, Samantha, "Clinton Asks Groups to Make Haiti Self-Sufficient," Associated Press, March 25, 2010.

Hadjadj, Bernard, *Education for All in Haiti over the Last 20 Years: Assessment and Perspectives*, Kingston, Jamaica: Office of the United Nations Educational, Scientific and Cultural Organization Representative in the Caribbean, monograph series 18, 2000.

Haiti: A New Paradigm, c. 2009. As of July 13, 2010 (choose Documents then Haiti Reference Document): http://events.iadb.org/calendar/eventDetail.aspx?source=press&lang=en&id=525

Haiti Reconstruction Platform, "Pledge List," undated web page. As of July 14, 2010: http://www.refondation.ht/index.jsp?sid=1&id=191&pid=126&lng=en

"Haitian National Police Reform Plan," attachment to United Nations Secretary-General, *Letter Dated 31 August 2006 from the Secretary-General Addressed to the President of the Security Council*, New York: United Nations, S/2006/726, September 12, 2006.

High Level Forum on Aid Effectiveness, *Paris Declaration on Aid Effectiveness*, Paris, February 28–March 2, 2005; adopted by Organisation for Economic Co-Operation and Development Development Assistance Committee Ministers, March 2, 2005. As of July 14, 2010:
http://www.oecd.org/dataoecd/11/41/34428351.pdf

"House, Senate Panel Leaders Unveil Haiti Preferences Deal," *Congressional Daily*, April 29, 2010.

IDB—*See* Inter-American Development Bank.

IHRC—*See* Interim Haiti Recovery Commission.

IHSI—*See* Institut Haïtien de Statistique et d'Informatique.

ILAC—*See* International Legal Assistance Consortium.

IMF—*See* International Monetary Fund.

Institut Haïtien de Statistique et d'Informatique, *Enquête sur les Conditions de Vie en Haïti*, Vol. II, Port-au-Prince: République d'Haïti, Ministère de l'économie et des Finances, July 2005. As of July 13, 2010:
http://www.ihsi.ht/pdf/ecvh/pnud_livre_enquete_volume_II.pdf

InterAction, *From the Ground Up: InterAction Member Recommendations on Recovery and Reconstruction in Haiti*, Washington, D.C., March 19, 2010. As of July 14, 2010:
http://www.interaction.org/document/
ground-interaction-member-recommendations-recovery-and-reconstruction-haiti

Inter-Agency Standing Committee, Haiti Shelter Cluster, minutes, April 27, 2010. As of July 14, 2010:
https://sites.google.com/site/shelterhaiti2010/minutes/
100427_SC_MEETING_Minutes2.doc

Inter-American Development Bank, *Country Program Evaluation: Haiti 2001–2006*, Washington, D.C.: Office of Evaluation and Oversight, RE-327, 2007. As of July 14, 2010:
http://www.iadb.org/ove/GetDocument.aspx?DOCNUM=1015148

———, *Haiti: Strengthening Public Finance Management II*, grant proposal, March 2008.

———, "Haiti Donors Conference: Toward a New Cooperation Paradigm for Growth and Opportunity," Washington, D.C., April 14, 2009. As of July 13, 2010:
http://events.iadb.org/calendar/eventDetail.aspx?source=press&lang=en&id=525

———, Reconstruction and Reorganization of Schools in Post-Earthquake Haiti, draft for discussion, February 2010.

Interim Haiti Recovery Commission, undated home page. As of July 21, 2010: http://www.cirh.ht/

International Crisis Group, *Haiti: Justice Reform and the Security Crisis*, Port-au-Prince, Latin American/Caribbean briefing 14, January 31, 2007a.

———, *Haiti: Prison Reform and the Rule of Law*, Port-au-Prince, Latin American/Caribbean briefing 15, May 4, 2007b.

———, *Reforming Haiti's Security Sector*, Washington, D.C., Latin American/Caribbean report 28, September 18, 2008.

———, *Haiti: Stabilisation and Reconstruction After the Quake*, Port-au-Prince, Latin America/Caribbean report 32, 2010. As of July 13, 2010: http://www.crisisgroup.org/en/regions/latin-america-caribbean/haiti/032-haiti-stabilisation-and-reconstruction-after-the-quake.aspx

International Donors' Conference Towards a New Future for Haiti, "Final Communiqué," March 31, 2010. As of July 14, 2010: http://www.haiticonference.org/communique.html

International Legal Assistance Consortium, *ILAC Report: Haiti*, Stockholm, January 2005. As of July 13, 2010: http://www.ilac.se/sites/default/files/Haiti_Report_2005.pdf

International Monetary Fund, "International Financial Statistics," undated website. As of July 13, 2010: http://www.imfstatistics.org/imf/

———, *Haiti: Request for a Three-Year Arrangement Under the Poverty Reduction and Growth Facility—Staff Report; Staff Press Release on the Executive Board Discussion; and Statement by the Executive Director for Haiti*, country report 06/441, December 2006.

———, *Haiti: Poverty Reduction Strategy Paper*, country report 08/115, March 2008. As of July 13, 2010: http://www.imf.org/external/pubs/ft/scr/2008/cr08115.pdf

———, *Haiti: Fifth Review Under the Three-Year Arrangement Under the Poverty Reduction and Growth Facility, and Request for Waiver of Performance Criterion, Modification of Performance Criteria, and Extension of the Arrangement—Staff Report; Press Release on the Executive Board Discussion; and Statement by the Executive Director for Haiti*, country report 09/258, August 2009a.

———, *Haiti: Joint Staff Advisory Note of the Annual Progress Report on Implementation of the Poverty Reduction Strategy Paper*, Washington, D.C., country report 09/289, August 2009b. As of July 13, 2010: http://bibpurl.oclc.org/web/37138/2009/cr09289.pdf

———, *Haiti: Sixth Review Under the Extended Credit Facility, Request for Waiver of Performance Criterion, and Augmentation of Access—Staff Report; Staff Statements; Press Release on the Executive Board Discussion; and Statement by the Executive Director for Haiti*, country report 10/35, February 2010.

International Trade Administration, U.S. Department of Commerce, "TradeStats™ Home," undated website. As of July 13, 2010:
http://tse.export.gov/TSE/TSEhome.aspx

Interuniversity Institute for Research and Development, *The Challenge for Haitian Higher Education: A Post-Earthquake Assessment of Higher Education Institutions in the Port-au-Prince Metropolitan Area*, Port-au-Prince, March 2010. As of July 14, 2010:
http://inured.org/docs/TheChallengeforHaitianHigherEd_INURED2010March.pdf

INURED—*See* Interuniversity Institute for Research and Development.

Jensen, Erik G., "Justice and the Rule of Law," in Charles Call, ed., with Vanessa Wyeth, *Building States to Build Peace*, Boulder, Colo.: Lynne Rienner Publishers, 2008, pp. 119–142.

Johnson, E. Thomas, "Haitian Government Is a Major Impediment to Relief Efforts," *Los Angeles Times*, July 8, 2010, p. 7A.

J-PAL—*See* Abdul Latif Jameel Poverty Action Lab.

Kaplan, Seth, "Fixing Fragile States," *Policy Review*, Vol. 152, December 2008a, pp. 63–77.

———, *Fixing Fragile States: A New Paradigm for Development*, Westport, Conn.: Praeger Security International, 2008b.

Kaufmann, Daniel, Aart Kraay, and Massimo Mastruzzi, *Governance Matters VII: Aggregate and Individual Governance Indicators, 1996–2007*, Washington, D.C.: World Bank, World Bank Institute, Global Programs Division, and Development Research Group, Macroeconomics and Growth Team, June 2008.

King's College London, "World Prison Brief," last modified June 7, 2010. As of July 13, 2010:
http://www.kcl.ac.uk/depsta/law/research/icps/worldbrief/

Krasner, Stephen D., and Carlos Pascual, "Addressing State Failure," *Foreign Affairs*, Vol. 84, No. 4, July–August 2005, pp. 153–163.

Kristof, Nicholas D., "Some Frank Talk About Haiti," *New York Times*, January 20, 2010, p. 7. As of July 13, 2010:
http://www.nytimes.com/2010/01/21/opinion/21kristof.html

Library of Congress, Federal Research Division, *Country Profile, Haiti*, Washington, D.C., May 2006. As of July 14, 2010:
http://lcweb2.loc.gov/frd/cs/profiles/Haiti.pdf

Lindsay, Reed, "Peace Despite the Peacekeepers in Haiti," *NACLA Report on the Americas*, Vol. 39, No. 6, May–June 2006, pp. 31–37.

Logistics Cluster, undated home page. As of July 14, 2010:
http://www.logcluster.org/

Malone, David, "A Lost Door to the Future," *Globe and Mail*, March 2, 2004.

Mendelson-Forman, Johanna, "Security Sector Reform in Haiti," *International Peacekeeping*, Vol. 13, No. 1, March 2006, pp. 14–27.

MENFP—*See* Ministère de l'Education Nationale et de la Formation Professionnelle.

Miguel, Edward, Shanker Satyanath, and Ernest Sergenti, "Economic Shocks and Civil Conflict: An Instrumental Variables Approach," *Journal of Political Economy*, Vol. 112, No. 4, August 2004, pp. 725–753.

Ministère de l'Education Nationale et de la Formation Professionnelle, *La Stratégie Nationale d'Action pour l'Education pour Tous*, September 1997.

———, *La Stratégie Nationale d'Action pour l'Education pour Tous*, September 2007. As of July 21, 2010:
http://planipolis.iiep.unesco.org/upload/Haiti/Haiti_EFA.pdf

———, *National Support Program for Back to School*, 2010a.

———, list of specialists in recruitment for strengthening the ministry, obtained from donor 1, May 2010b.

Ministère de la Justice et de la Sécurité Publique, Police Nationale d'Haïti, Direction de l'Administration Pénitentiaire, five-year plan, 2006–2011, c. 2006.

———, *Plan de Développement Stratégique 2007–2012*, c. 2007.

Ministère de la Santé Publique et de la Population, *Strategic Plan for Health Sector Reform*, March 2004.

———, *Plan Intérimaire du Secteur Santé, Mars 2010–Septembre 2011*, c. 2010.

Mintz, Sidney W., "Can Haiti Change?" *Foreign Affairs*, Vol. 74, No. 1, January–February 1995, pp. 73–86.

MINUSTAH—*See* United Nations Stabilization Mission in Haiti.

MJSP—*See* Ministère de la Justice et de la Sécurité Publique.

Mobekk, Eirin, "MINUSTAH and the Need for a Context-Specific Strategy: The Case of Haiti," in Heiner Hänggi and Vincenza Scherrer, eds., *Security Sector Reform and UN Integrated Missions: Experience from Burundi, the Democratic Republic of Congo, Haiti and Kosovo*, Berlin: Lit, 2008, pp. 113–168.

Morley, Morris, and Chris McGillion, "'Disobedient' Generals and the Politics of Redemocratization: The Clinton Administration and Haiti," *Political Science Quarterly*, Vol. 112, No. 3, Autumn 1997, pp. 363–384.

MSPP—*See* Ministère de la Santé Publique et de la Population.

Nathan Associates, *Bringing HOPE to Haiti's Apparel Industry: Improving Competitiveness Through Factory-Level Value-Chain Analysis*, Commission Tripartite de la Mise en Oeuvre de la Loi HOPE, November 2009. As of July 13, 2010:
http://apps.ubmasia.com/files/mediaobjects/Files/25/PSF/10%20WB%20Haiti%20Apparel%20Industry.pdf

OAS—*See* Organization of American States.

OECD—*See* Organisation for Economic Co-Operation and Development.

Office of the United Nations Special Envoy for Haiti, "Lessons Learned from the Tsunami," undated web page. As of July 14, 2010:
http://www.haitispecialenvoy.org/tsunami_lessons

———, *Key Propositions for Building Back Better: Lessons Learned from Tsunami Recovery—A Report by the United Nations Secretary-General's Special Envoy for Tsunami Recovery, William J. Clinton*, December 2006. As of July 14, 2010:
http://ochaonline.un.org/OchaLinkClick.aspx?link=ocha&docid=1005912

———, *A Voice for the Voiceless (Youn Vwa Pou Pep La): An Initiative to Include the Haitian People's Views for the 31 March 2010 Donor's Conference*, March 15, 2010. As of July 21, 2010 (choose Documents then Documents in English then Report on Voice of the Voiceless_English.pdf):
http://www.haiticonference.org/documents.html

Organisation for Economic Co-Operation and Development, *Principes pour l'Engagement International dans les États Fragiles*, Geneva, undated (a). As of July 13, 2010:
http://www.oecd.org/document/46/0,3343,fr_2649_33693550_39251440_1_1_1_1,00.html

———, "QWIDS: Query Wizard for International Development Statistics," undated (b) website. As of July 14, 2010:
http://stats.oecd.org/qwids/

———, *Geographical Distribution of Financial Flows to Developing Countries: Disbursements, Commitments, Country Indicators 2003–2007*, Paris, February 2009.

Organization of American States, *Haitian Diaspora Forum: Contributing to a Strategic Plan for Reconstruction and Development in Haiti*, Washington, D.C., March 21–23, 2010. As of July 14, 2010:
http://www.oas.org/en/news/haiti_earthquake_relief/haiti_earthquake_relief.asp

PAHO—*See* Pan American Health Organization.

Pan American Health Organization, "Haiti Earthquake: Health Q&As," undated web page. As of July 14, 2010:
http://new.paho.org/disasters/index.php?option=com_content&task=view&id=1104&Itemid=1

———, *Haiti: Profile of the Health Services System*, Program on Organization and Management of Health Systems and Service, Division of Health Systems and Services Development, June 2003.

———, *Health in the Americas, 2007*, 2007.

———, "Haiti: Population Health Assessment Prior to the 2010 Earthquake," January 21, 2010a. As of July 14, 2010:
http://new.paho.org/disasters/index.php?option=com_docman&task=doc_download&gid=689&Itemid=

———, "Earthquake in Haiti: The Response of the Pan American Health Organization/World Health Organization," updated March 3, 2010b.

PDNA—*See* Republic of Haiti (2010b).

Perito, Robert, and Jasenka Jocic, *Paper Versus Steel: Haiti's Challenge of Constitutional Reform*, Washington, D.C.: U.S. Institute of Peace, January 2008.

Private Sector Economic Forum, *Vision and Roadmap for Haiti*, draft, March 16, 2010.

Przeworski, Adam, *Democracy and the Market: Political and Economic Reforms in Eastern Europe and Latin America*, Cambridge: Cambridge University Press, 1991.

Public Law 106-200, Caribbean Basin Trade Partnership Act, May 18, 2000.

Public Law 110-246, Food, Conservation, and Energy Act of 2008, June 18, 2008. As of July 21, 2010:
http://frwebgate.access.gpo.gov/cgi-bin/getdoc.cgi?dbname=110_cong_public_laws&docid=f:publ246.110.pdf

Putnam, Robert D., with Robert Leonardi and Raffaella Nanetti, *Making Democracy Work: Civic Traditions in Modern Italy*, Princeton, N.J.: Princeton University Press, 1993.

Republic of Haiti, *Interim Cooperation Framework 2004–2006: Summary Report*, July 2004. As of July 13, 2010:
http://haiticci.undg.org/uploads/ReportVersion8%20Eng%20FINAL%20Low%20Res.pdf

———, *Programme-Cadre de Réforme de l'Etat: Modernisation Administrative et Décentralisation, 2007–2012*, c. 2007.

———, Preparatory Committee for Growth and Poverty Reduction Strategy Paper, Technical Secretariat, *Growth and Poverty Reduction Strategy Paper (GPRSP) (2008–2010): Making a Qualitative Leap Forward [Document de Stratégie Nationale pour la Croissance et pour la Réduction de la Pauvreté (DSNCRP)]*, Washington, D.C.: International Monetary Fund, 2008. As of July 13, 2010: http://www.mpce.gouv.ht/dsrp.htm

———, *Action Plan for National Recovery and Development of Haiti: Immediate Key Initiatives for the Future*, Port-au-Prince: Government of the Republic of Haiti, March 2010a. As of July 13, 2010: http://haiticonference.org/Haiti_Action_Plan_ENG.pdf

———, *Haiti Earthquake PDNA: Assessment of Damage, Losses, General and Sectoral Needs, annex to Action Plan for National Recovery and Development of Haiti: Immediate Key Initiatives for the Future*, Port-au-Prince: Government of the Republic of Haiti, March 2010b. Official version, in French, as of July 14, 2010: http://www.reliefweb.int/rw/RWFiles2010.nsf/FilesByRWDocUnidFilename/SNAA-83U9QH-rapport_complet.pdf/$File/rapport_complet.pdf

Roper, Laura, with Emily Utz and John Harvey, *The Tsunami Learning Project: Lessons for Grantmakers in Natural Disaster Response*, Grantmakers Without Borders, 2006. As of July 14, 2010: http://www.gwob.net/issues/pdf/tlp_full-report.pdf

Rotberg, Robert I., ed., *State Failure and State Weakness in a Time of Terror*, Cambridge, Mass.: World Peace Foundation, 2003.

———, ed., *When States Fail: Causes and Consequences*, Princeton, N.J.: Princeton University Press, 2004.

Salmi, J., "Equity and Quality in Private Education: The Haitian Paradox," in *Haiti: The Challenges of Poverty Reduction*, Vol. II: *Technical Papers*, World Bank, report 17242-HA, March 1998, pp. 1–17.

Stephens, Matthew, "The Commission on Legal Empowerment of the Poor: An Opportunity Missed," *Hague Journal on the Rule of Law*, Vol. 1, 2009, pp. 132–155.

Taft-Morales, Maureen, *Haiti: Current Conditions and Congressional Concerns*, Washington, D.C.: Congressional Research Service, Library of Congress, R40507, 2009.

Taft-Morales, Maureen, and Rhoda Margesson, *Haiti Earthquake: Crisis and Response*, Washington, D.C.: Congressional Research Service, January 15, 2010. As of July 13, 2010: http://handle.dtic.mil/100.2/ADA513517

Transparency International, *Corruption Perceptions Index*, 2009. As of July 13, 2010: http://www.transparency.org/policy_research/surveys_indices/cpi/2009

"UN Special Envoy Says Haiti in Urgent Need of Police, Judicial Reform," *BBC Monitoring Latin America*, March 28, 2006.

UNDG—*See* United Nations Development Group.

UNDP—*See* United Nations Development Programme.

UNESCO—*See* United Nations Educational, Scientific and Cultural Organization.

United Nations Department of Peacekeeping Operations, "4 March, 2010: Momentum at UN Continues to Help Haiti Rebuild Institutions," undated web page. As of July 13, 2010:
http://www.un.int/wcm/content/lang/en/pid/15017

United Nations Development Group, *Haiti PCNA Case Study*, October 2006. As of July 21, 2010:
http://www.undg.org/archive_docs/8884-Haiti_PCNA_Case_Study.doc

United Nations Development Programme, *2002–2008, Haiti—Outcome 7: Rule of Law, Justice, and Human Rights*, August 2003. As of July 13, 2010:
http://erc.undp.org/evaluationadmin/manageevaluation/viewevaluationdetail.html?evalid=1341

———, *Human Development Report 2009, M: Economy and Inequality*, c. 2009. As of July 13, 2010:
http://hdrstats.undp.org/en/indicators/161.html

United Nations Educational, Scientific and Cultural Organization, *CR of the April 16 Meeting on Important Steps to Be Taken Before the Joint Donor Education in June 2010*, May 2010.

United Nations Secretary-General, *Letter Dated 2006/08/17 from the Secretary-General Addressed to the President of the Security Council*, New York: United Nations, S/2006/626, 2006.

United Nations Security Council, resolution 1542, April 30, 2004a.

———, *Report of the Secretary-General on the United Nations Stabilization Mission in Haiti*, S/2004/908, October 2004b.

———, *Report of the Secretary-General on the United Nations Stabilization Mission in Haiti*, S/2005/631, October 2005.

———, *Report of the Secretary-General on the United Nations Stabilization Mission in Haiti*, New York, March 26, 2008.

———, *Report of the Secretary-General on the United Nations Stabilization Mission in Haiti*, New York, March 6, 2009a.

———, *Report of the Secretary-General on the United Nations Stabilization Mission in Haiti*, S/2009/439, September 1, 2009b.

———, resolution 1908 (2010), S/RES/1908, January 19, 2010.

United Nations Stabilization Mission in Haiti, "MINUSTAH Facts and Figures," undated web page. As of July 7, 2010:
http://www.un.org/en/peacekeeping/missions/minustah/facts.shtml

United Nations Statistics Division, "Millennium Development Goals Indicators," undated website. As of July 13, 2010:
http://mdgs.un.org/unsd/mdg/Data.aspx

UNSC—*See* United Nations Security Council.

UNSD—*See* United Nations Statistics Division.

U.S. Department of State, Under Secretary for Political Affairs, Bureau of International Narcotics and Law Enforcement Affairs, Office of Civilian Police and Rule of Law Programs, "Civilian Police Programs," undated web page. As of July 13, 2010:
http://www.state.gov/p/inl/civ/c27153.htm

U.S. General Accounting Office, *Foreign Assistance: Any Further Aid to Haitian Justice System Should Be Linked to Performance-Related Conditions*, Washington, D.C., GAO-01-24, October 2000. As of July 13, 2010:
http://purl.access.gpo.gov/GPO/LPS12237

Vallas, Paul, *Haitian Education Recovery Plan: Preliminary Draft*, 2010.

Varma, Monika Kalra, "Haiti Donors Conference: A New Paradigm or New Packaging?" *Huffington Post*, April 19, 2009. As of July 13, 2010:
http://www.huffingtonpost.com/monika-kalra-varma/haiti-donors-conference-a_b_188786.html

Von Amsberg, Joachim, "Out of Aceh's Experience, Hope for Rebuilding Haiti," *Washington Post*, January 29, 2010. As of July 14, 2010:
http://www.washingtonpost.com/wp-dyn/content/article/2010/01/28/AR2010012803561.html

Weingast, Barry R., "The Political Foundations of Democracy and the Rule of Law," *American Political Science Review*, Vol. 91, No. 2, June 1997, pp. 245–263.

Wente, Margaret, "Is Haiti Hopeless? Can We 'Fix' It?" *Globe and Mail*, March 5, 2010, last updated March 11, 2010, p. A25. As of July, 13, 2010:
http://www.theglobeandmail.com/news/opinions/is-haiti-hopeless-can-we-fix-it/article1491967/

WHO—*See* World Health Organization.

Wolff, Laurence, *Education in Haiti: The Way Forward*, Washington, D.C.: Programa de Promoción de la Reforma Educativa de America Latina y el Caribe, September 26, 2008. As of July 14, 2010:
http://www.thedialogue.org/page.cfm?pageID=32&pubID=1605

World Bank, *Damage, Loss and Preliminary Needs Assessment: Executive Summary*, undated (a). As of July 14, 2010:
http://siteresources.worldbank.org/INTINDONESIA/Resources/Publication/280016-1235115695188/5847179-1257228519234/exsum.en.pdf

———, "Explore Economies: Haiti," undated web page (b). As of July 14, 2010:
http://www.doingbusiness.org/ExploreEconomies/?economyid=85

———, "Our Goal: Education for All in Haiti," undated web page (c). As of July 14, 2010:
http://web.worldbank.org/WBSITE/EXTERNAL/COUNTRIES/LACEXT/0,,contentMDK:21896642~pagePK:146736~piPK:146830~print:Y~theSitePK:258554,00.html

———, "Paying Taxes in Haiti," undated web page (d). As of July 14, 2010:
http://www.doingbusiness.org/ExploreTopics/PayingTaxes/Details.aspx?economyid=85

———, International Economics Department, Development Data Group, *World Development Indicators*, Washington, D.C., undated website (e). As of July 14, 2010:
http://bibpurl.oclc.org/web/309

———, Operations Evaluation Department, *Haiti: Country Assistance Evaluation*, Washington, D.C., report 23637-HA, 2002.

———, "Brazil Funds Haiti's National School Feeding Program: Grant Agreement Signed as Part of World Bank Post Conflict Fund Grant," press release 2005/252/LAC, December 20, 2004. As of July 14, 2010:
http://web.worldbank.org/WBSITE/EXTERNAL/NEWS/0,,contentMDK:20297736~pagePK:34370~piPK:34424~theSitePK:4607,00.html

———, *Haiti: Social Resilience and State Fragility in Haiti: A Country Social Analysis*, Washington, D.C., report 36069-HT, April 27, 2006.

———, *Project Paper on a Proposed Grant in the Amount of SDR 12.8Million (US$ 20Million Equivalent) to the Republic of Haiti for an Emergency Bridge Reconstruction and Vulnerability Reduction Project*, report 46121-HA, November 3, 2008a. As of July 14, 2010:
http://www-wds.worldbank.org/external/default/WDSContentServer/WDSP/IB/2008/11/12/000333038_20081112024924/Rendered/PDF/461210PJPR0P111LY10IDA1R20081029811.pdf

———, *Data Sheet: Project Paper: Transport and Territorial Development Project—Project Restructuring*, report 46844, November 19, 2008b. As of July 14, 2010:
http://www-wds.worldbank.org/external/default/WDSContentServer/WDSP/IB/2008/12/14/000333037_20081214225301/Rendered/PDF/468440PJPR0P091URING0IDA1R200810320.pdf

———, "Governance Matters 2009: Worldwide Governance Indicators, 1996–2008," c. 2009a. As of July 13, 2010:
http://info.worldbank.org/governance/wgi/sc_chart.asp

———, *Project Paper on a Proposed Additional Grant in the Amount of SDR 3.3 Million to the Republic of Haiti for the Electricity Loss Reduction Project*, report 49402-HT, July 29, 2009b.

———, *Haiti at a Glance*, September 12, 2009c. As of July 14, 2010:
http://devdata.worldbank.org/AAG/hti_aag.pdf

———, *Status of Projects in Execution—FY09 SOPE, Operations Policy and Country Services*, October 2, 2009d. As of July 14, 2010:
http://web.worldbank.org/WBSITE/EXTERNAL/PROJECTS/EXTSOPE/0,,menuPK:5929632~pagePK:64168427~piPK:64168435~theSitePK:5929621,00.html

World Food Programme, *Earthquake in Haiti: External Situation Report*, March 6, 2010. As of July 14, 2010:
http://home.wfp.org/stellent/groups/public/documents/newsroom/wfp214946.pdf

World Health Organization, "Welcome to the Global Health Observatory," undated website. As of July 14, 2010:
http://apps.who.int/ghodata/

Zoellick, Robert B., "Fragile States: Securing Development," *Survival*, Vol. 50, No. 6, December 2008, pp. 67–84.